AS FATE WOULD HAVE IT

As Fate Would Have It

Tom Jefferson, MD

LUMINARE PRESS

WWW.LUMINAREPRESS.COM

Luminare Press
442 Charnelton
Eugene, OR 97401
www.luminarepress.com

LCCN: 2019913831
ISBN: 978-1-64388-196-6

*My life has been an adventure, and continues to be;
I wouldn't trade it in on any other scenario. I had my
differences with my mother and father, as outlined within.
But they loved me, and provided the opportunity and
freedom to live out my natural inclinations.*

*Most importantly, they demonstrated to my sister Betty
and I that they loved each other, that loving someone was
possible, and that despite difficulties in their own early lives,
love lay waiting to express itself. It gives me great joy
to see that live on in our family.*

Love creates love. I wish it for all.

*So to you, George and Martha Jefferson, thanks for the
opportunity to experience the wonders of life,
and all that comes with it.*

Some things are up to us, others are not.

—Epictetus

Contents

I seem to have inherited the desire to write from my mother and father. My mother wrote of her early years in *The Attic of my Mind*, and published a cookbook, *Chicken Ever' Sunday*. After the war my father wrote of his B-29 squadron's experiences while stationed in Saipan, then wrote the definitive *Right of Way Negotiation Team* article that landed him the job that allowed him to send my sister and I to college. He devoured murder mysteries, then one day slammed a finished mystery forcefully and declared, "I can write better than this," and proceeded to start writing his own Mike Hammer-like mystery, finding out how hard it actually was after five chapters.

I had no idea other than to write stories to describe vivid and meaningful memories from my life. Thus, the chapters are not necessarily in chronological order; each is meant to stand on its own and may span several decades.

These vignettes were written over the course of a year and a half, with the support, critiques and edits of a small memoir writing class, led by editor Cecilia Hagen.

There is a mix of life events, medical tales, and influences.

I hope you enjoy it.

War And Peace

In 1963, when I was not quite fifteen, our family moved from central Texas to northern Virginia. While unpacking, I came across our large family bible, a hardcover 1881 Jones Brothers Self-Interpreting Pictorial Family Bible. It was inscribed to Thomas Vandivier (Big Dad, my mother's grandfather, who I was named after), and his wife Martha Hasseltine Roe (who my mother Martha was named after). The Bible had been brought by wagon from Georgia to Texas in the 1880s and had now accompanied us to Virginia.

When I was younger, I had been captivated by the bible's full-page black-and-white engravings protected by thin sheets of transparent glassine paper. In particular, I was struck by the picture of Sampson destroying the pillars, and David holding Goliath's severed head in triumph. These pictures had once induced wonder, and I paused to lose myself in them again.

Samson

David and Goliath

    As Fate Would Have It

As I flipped through the Bible, I encountered two items that struck me in a way that changed my life.

Between the Old and New Testament was a section dedicated to the entry of family names. There, inked by an unknown hand in beautiful but fading script, were the birth, marriage, and death dates of a few family members. Photographs of some of these people had hung in our house for years. It had always fascinated me to think that these old-timey looking people, the long-bearded men and the women in their high-necked, full-skirted Sunday best clothes were my relatives. I wondered what their lives had been like and was particularly fascinated by the simple summary of a person's life, as in, *T.A. Vandivier (1844-1927)*. I wandered in this biblical paper cemetery, visualizing past eras.

Martha "Hassie" Roe (1847–1918) and
T.A. Vandiver (1844–1927)

Jane Elam Roe (Hassie's Mother) 1813–1893

But then I found, nestled in the pages of the Epistle to the Romans, a piece of yellowed and brittle paper. I carefully unfolded it to find a 100-year-old letter, written in careful script, by Big Dad and his brother James, when they were eighteen and twenty-two years old. They were writing to their family in Georgia from a winter encampment along Virginia's Rappahannock River following the Battle of Fredericksburg, in 1863, during the Civil War.

Camp Near Frederaksburg, VA.

January 26TH, 1863

Dear Ser

I this eavning take the opportunity to drop you a few lines to let you know that me and Tom ise well at present, hoping these few lines may find you and your family well. We received your letter the 25th. I was glad to hear from you all. Your letter sed that a log fell on you and hurt you but you was agetting better. I am as fat and harty as you every saw me.

We are hear in the woods without enny tents yet alooking for a big fight every day but we are well fortified heare. We have been a fortyfing every sence the Frederaksburg fight. We have a heap of work to do heare a throing up brest works. We are on one side of the river and the Yanks are on the other side. We can see them plane enough across the river. We can hollow over and talk to them enny time we please. I want you to write how you are agetting along and how times are there. I want you to write to us every chance. Times is hard heare so must come to close.

Direct your letter to Richmond and I will get them care of Captain Adams (Co) (L) (28) Ga. Vol.

* * *

James Vandivier

I want you to tell Aunt Couis how to Dyrect her letery to me. I wrote her a lear to Day and did forget to tel her how to Dyrect her leter to me and I want you to write me. I wrote you a leter a good whole weak

My excitement was uncontained. A personal family letter
from a Civil War battlefield! I was taken by the spelling
and dialect, and immediately began to picture James and
Tom writing in their primitive camp. The adolescent anxiety generated by my family's move from Texas to Virginia
evaporated in the germination of a new obsession.

I had always been intrigued by war. As a child, I played
with my father's WWII knapsack, ammo belt, canteen, and
aviators' hat, and marveled over his military medals. He
wrote of his experiences as navigator/radar operator in B-29s
flying the last missions of WWII over Japan. I read his war
diary, mostly filled with tales of off-duty poker and movies,
and the trading of beer rations, cigarettes, and whisky. I had
armies of plastic soldiers with which I staged grand battles
in the living room. I watched every war movie shown on
television. I play-acted fighting alongside imaginary others
who would live or die and understood deeply that war risked
death. I practiced war, should it ever come to that for me.

Growing up in Texas, the only history taught, or at least
all I remembered, was Texas war history—the Alamo, San
Jacinto, Goliad, Stephen F. Austin, Sam Houston, Jim Bowie,
Davy Crockett. Our family vacationed at Texas battle sites.
I had relatives who were Texas Rangers. Even though I was
forbidden to have even a BB gun, I pictured myself riding
a horse across the Texas plains while galloping after bad
guys, shooting a Colt .45.

But I knew next to nothing about the Civil War. And now, in Virginia, I was reading a 100-year-old letter that had been written by relatives from a Civil War battle site that was only an hour's drive away.

Sensing my enthusiasm, my mother related a Civil War story about her grandmother, Martha Hasseltine (Hassie) Roe, who later married Thomas (Big Dad) Vandiver. During Sherman's war-ending scorched-earth march through Georgia, a patrol of Union soldiers, under orders to forage from and psychologically intimidate civilians, came upon Hassie's home. One of them went into the attic and brought down a dresser drawer of her brother's clothes, he being off to war. Picking up a red-hot poker from the fire, Hassie warned the soldiers that they would be taking her brother's clothes over her dead body, yelling "I'd rather die a quick pain than a slow fever." Apparently, that was that, as they left with only the empty dresser drawers to use as troughs to feed their horses, chuckling about the "Little Rebel," as she heard them call her.

* * *

ARMED WITH THE FADED LETTER, SOME STORIES, AND A genealogical start from the ancestral bible, I was determined to find out everything I could about the Vandivers and their Roe cousins during the Civil War. I was compelled to know what their lives were like, obsessed with recreating and reliving their war experiences.

Accessing such information before the Internet was much harder than it is now. As I devoured magazines and books to understand the Battle of Fredericksburg, I discovered that if you knew the company and regiment of a Civil War soldier, you could find monthly musters, or regiment roll-calls, on microfilm at the National Archives. I began almost daily bus trips to the Civil War microfilm rooms in Washington, D.C., now only thirty minutes away. This allowed me to research what battles they participated in throughout the Civil War. Over a period of weeks, I tracked the entire chronology and whereabouts of five of my relatives through the Civil War (you can do that in hours now over the internet). I researched the history of troop movements, and the role my relatives would have played in those battles. The historical record of the positions of each regiment, company, and division during battles is archived in exhaustive detail. This stimulated me, as a teenager, to write up what I discovered into a forty-page narrative, which I proudly entitled, *The Whereabouts of Privates Thomas A. and James J. Vandiver, 28th Regiment, Georgia Volunteers; and of Privates John L., Jesse M., and Captain Isaac A. Roe, 19th Regiment, Georgia Volunteers.*

My research and writing uncovered an extraordinary story. James Vandiver never returned from the Civil War. His family presumed him dead, but they never knew exactly what happened to him. One hundred years later, in a reading room at the National Archives, I found out. He had been wounded and captured in October 1864 in Walker County, Georgia. He developed pneumonia and was taken to a Union hospital in Louisville, then was sent by steamboat up the Mississippi River to Chicago, where he was admitted to the major Union prisoner-of-war facility, Camp Douglas. Conditions were grim in the camp, with poor sanitation and nutrition, crowded conditions, and freezing temperatures. Thousands of prisoners died; the story is memorialized in the documentary *"80 Acres of Hell."* Shortly after imprisonment, he was admitted to the hospital with pneumonia, and

     As Fate Would Have It

then developed scurvy. In July 1865, after nine months in captivity, the now twenty-four-year-old James Vandiver died of tuberculosis. Sadly, he died three months after the Civil War had ended.

To my further astonishment, the death report showed the Chicago graveyard and gravesite number where he was buried! My mother gave me the addresses of his relatives still living in Georgia, and I wrote them to tell them that I had finally discovered what had happened to Uncle James during the Civil War. They were of course most grateful and equally amazed that you could find out such a thing, one hundred years later.

I hoped to visit his gravesite, to pay my respects to great grand-uncle James Vandiver, who, with the letter to his family, had started me on this journey. But I learned that shortly after the war, Lake Michigan catastrophically flooded, washing bodies from the prison hospital cemetery into the lake. The bodies had been reburied in a mass grave, known as the Confederate Mound, which exists to this day in Chicago's Oak Woods Cemetery. I may still go there some day, but the thought of visiting a mass grave is somehow less appealing.

(Confederate.) _Ga_

_V._ | _28_ | _Ala._

James Vandiver.

Pri., Co. _I_, _28_ Reg't _Ala._

Appears on a

Report

of prisoners of war who have died at General Hospital, Camp Douglas, Ill., from July 15 to July 31, 1865.

Report dated ______________________

Not dated, 186 .

Where captured ______________________

When captured ______________________, 186 .

When joined ~~station~~ _Hospl_ _July 9_, 1865 .

Died _July 9_, 1865 .

Cause of death _Phthisis Pulmonalis._

Number of grave _1190._

Locality of grave _Chicago City_

Cemetery.

NOTE: The patients in the Prison Hospital were transferred to the General Hospital July 9, and the Prison Hospital was closed from that date by order of the Commissary General of Prisoners.

Remarks: ______________________

____

____

____

Number of roll:

315; sheet ______ _W. Hay Scott,_

(654) Copyist.

James Vandiver Death Notice, Camp Douglas, July 9, 1865

To determine the conditions and circumstances under which James and my great-grandfather Thomas wrote the letter, I researched the winter of 1862-1863, when the two armies of the Civil War camped across the Rappahannock River from each other. The North and South took a break from fighting to regroup after the horrific five-day Battle of Fredericksburg, fought the previous month, where 200,000 American men fought each other and 18,000 died, were wounded, or missing. The "time-out" allowed armies to bury the dead, exchange prisoners of war, and rethink strategy and supply lines.

That winter was cold, and conditions were poor. When James declared *"I am as fat and harty as you every saw me,"* he was most surely lying to boost the spirits of his family back home, as he later intimates when he writes *"Times is hard heare…"* When he said, *"we are on one side of the river and the Yanks are on the other side,…we can hollow over and talk to them enny time we please,"* he was referring to an unofficial wintertime truce between the foot soldiers of the two armies.

Many stories survived this winter. Soldiers from opposing armies would send small boats across the river, trading corn and tobacco for coffee, sugar, and pork, in a battlefield Christmas gift exchange. Each army had a band to boost spirits, and on Christmas there was a battle of the bands across the river. As the playing of the well-known but more emotional strains of Auld Lang Syne had been banned by the Union Army to combat despondency and desertion after their recent defeat at Fredericksburg, both sides of the river united in playing and singing the more upbeat Home Sweet Home.

Mid pleasures and palaces though we may roam
Be it ever so humble, there's no place like home
A charm from the skies seems to hallow us there
Which seek thro' the world, is ne'er met elsewhere
Home! Home!
Sweet, sweet home!
There's no place like home
There's no place like home!

An exile from home splendor dazzles in vain
Oh give me my lowly thatched cottage again
The birds singing gaily that came at my call
And gave me the peace of mind dearer than all
Home, home, sweet, sweet home
There's no place like home, there's no place like home!

Big Dad survived and finally did make it back to Home
Sweet Home, after Confederate soldiers were pardoned by
Abraham Lincoln.

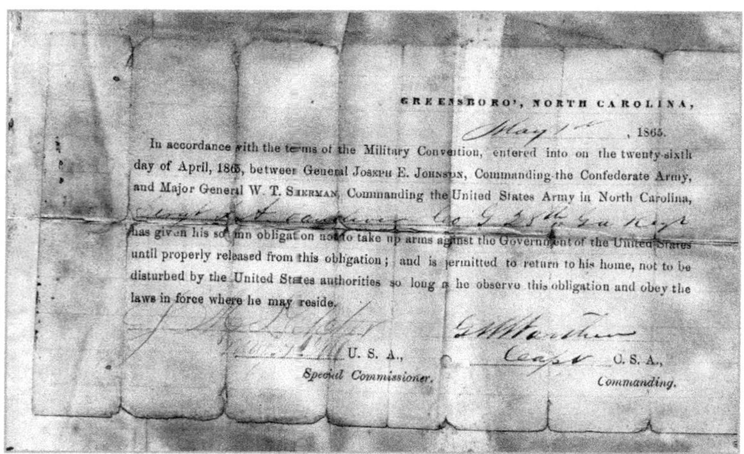

T. A. Vandiver Civil War Parole

   As Fate Would Have It

The research I did as a teenager showed me there was an entire world of family records that could provide a link to the past, giving me a better understanding of the events and circumstances that led to, well, me. After all, had it been Great Grandpa Thomas instead of Uncle James who was wounded and died, there would be no me writing this down, now 150 years later.

*　*　*

MY INTEREST IN GENEALOGY EXTENDED BEYOND WAR history, and I began researching other ancestors' stories. The other side of my mother's family were the Renshaws. I once asked my mother, "What part of the family do I take after?" "Well Tom," she said, "there's the Renshaw nose, and the Renshaw walk, and you've got 'em both." Her comment compelled me to investigate the Renshaws, and that too was an interesting journey through census and birth records, and preserved histories of the times.

The Renshaws came from England to Maryland in the 1600s, lived there for a few generations, then followed the Great Migration Highway from Maryland to North Carolina, where they settled in the late 1700s in the piedmont region of northwestern North Carolina. There, on the banks of the Yadkin River, hundreds of families settled. The still existing plot map shows g-g-g-g-g-g-Grandfather Abraham Renshaw's land adjacent to that of Squire Boone, father of Daniel Boone. Could my relatives have known Daniel Boone? If so, what did they think of him? As I had read biographies of Boone when I was much younger, I already had a mental picture of life on the Yadkin.

After I moved to Oregon, a fellow genealogy buff told me she was a documented descendant of Daniel Boone.

Knowing my family history, I showed her the North Carolina plot map, and we marveled at the web of life, our relatives having lived next door to each other 200 years ago, and
3000 miles away. From that moment we became kin-fellows,
which brought us pleasantly closer than we had been, even
though we were not directly related. As far as we knew.

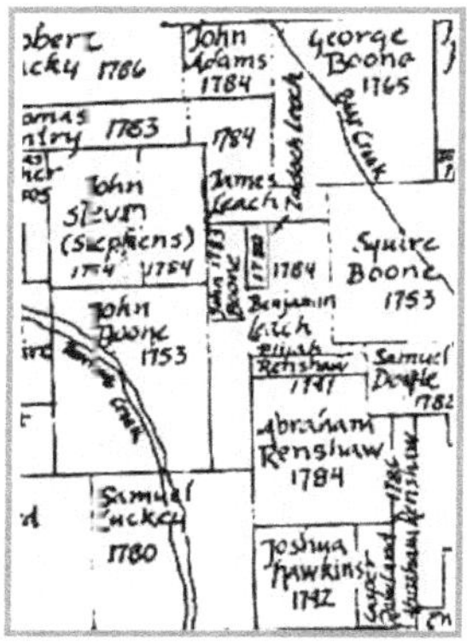

Plot Map near Salisbury, N.C., circa 1795

In the early 1800s the North Carolina Renshaws moved
to Illinois, where g-g-g-grandfather James Renshaw helped
found Decatur, Illinois, and was Decatur's first businessman.
In 1829 James, known as "Uncle Jimmy" by the locals, opened
a tavern, store, post office, pharmacy, and water-powered
sawmill, known as Renshaw's Mill. It was there he became
acquainted with the Lincoln family – Tom, Sarah, and their
son Abe. Abe split logs at the Renshaw mill, but that wasn't all.

Carl Sandburg, in the first chapter of *Abraham Lincoln,
the Prairie Years*, writes of Abe's wilderness beginnings.

"…It was a change from the monotony of hard farm work in that summer of 1830 for Abraham to make his first political speech in Illinois. He had been delivering speeches to trees, stumps, rows of corn and potatoes, just practicing by himself. But when two legislative candidates spoke at a campaign meeting in front of Renshaw's store in Decatur, Abraham stepped up and advocated improvement of the Sangamon River for better navigation.

Fall came and most of the Lincoln family came down with chills, fever, and ague, Tom and Sarah using many doses of a quinine and whisky tonic mixture from a Decatur store…"

The store was Uncle Jimmy's store! Did g-g-g grandfather Jimmy Renshaw save Abe Lincoln's life and change the course of history? These are the kinds of unexpected speculative pleasures that emerge from the often-tedious work of family history research.

* * *

OVER THE YEARS, I CONTINUED TO RESEARCH THE RENshaws, Vandivers, and Jeffersons. About twenty years ago, I was online researching a branch of the Renshaws that came by covered wagon to Oregon instead of moving to Texas, when I came across a researcher knowledgeable about the Renshaws of Eugene, Oregon, where I was now living. The Renshaws of Eugene, Oregon! What?

A few clicks on the Internet, and I was having an email discussion with Steve Dillard, whose relatives married the Renshaws back in the 1860s. He told me there were Renshaws buried in the Masonic Cemetery in Eugene, which

was only two blocks away from where I sat! I dropped everything, literally ran over to the cemetery, and sure enough, I
found multiple Renshaw graves. At that time I was a runner,
and often ran through the paths of that cemetery, never
knowing I was running right by the grave sites of Renshaw
family members! The world is small, and occasionally
exhilaratingly revealing, when you know the details.

The Vandiver and Renshaw lines migrated to Texas,
where they joined to produce my mother, their only child,
in 1915. In 1938, the lines split, as Jessie Vandiver Renshaw
divorced her husband Holly Renshaw, on the grounds that

*"…while she was at all times kind and affectionate, and
performed her duties as a dutiful wife, that he began a course
of cruel and unkind treatment; that he declined to accompany
her to church or social gatherings, which was very embarrassing and caused her friends to gossip, and that he would
keep company of women of questionable character, and on
weekends would leave home and not return for a day or two,
and would refuse to advise her of his whereabouts and with
whom he was associating; and finally, though she continued
to prepare meals for him, he refused to carry on any kind of
conversation with her, and totally ignored her."*

My mother kept, then solemnly presented the divorce
papers to me, with a vague, brief, and tearfully delivered
recollection of how hard her childhood had been, and how
difficult it had been for she and my father to be parents,
since neither of them felt confident in their own parenting.
It was a rare demonstration of regret, that she felt obligated
to pass on to me; a poignant story that required no research,
just recollecting the past.

The last Renshaw relative I knew was my grandfather
Holly. Even though he lived in our same town, I rarely saw

him, and had no insight as a child as to why. I either did not know of my grandparents' separation or didn't remember what I was told. It didn't seem odd or important to me. My only real memory of him was the one and only time he was allowed to keep me for the day; he took me to gamble with his buddies at the domino hall. I had a great time, but he apparently lost child-care privileges after that. Even though the Vandivers and Renshaws ultimately didn't get along, in better times, Holly and Jessie produced my mother, and ultimately me, and my interest in their families' stories.

* * *

I AM GRATEFUL TO HAVE LEARNED THESE STORIES. MY life feels richer as a result of learning about my relatives' travels, their successes and failures, and the stories that are still told about them. I now "know" relatives I never met. It has been a satisfying jigsaw puzzle to put together, linking bits and pieces of stories, letters, photographs, discoveries, and handed-down family treasures, each with their own story. I love knowing these stories, and enjoy my role documenting them as completely as I can, so I can continue the tradition of passing them along to future generations.

And, it inspired me to tell some of my own stories.

B Flat

⁂

I was singing, or at least I was supposed to be. I can't recall any sound. The studio lights were hot and blinding. A huge monster with a large red eye was moving slowly toward me, with a hazy audience behind, watching. A man began sweeping the floor around me. I was sweating, over-stimulated, terrified.

This was not a bad dream. It was show biz, my career before elementary school. The monster was a TV camera. The red light's meaning was "you are on-air." As in, "Live, from WBAP-TV in Fort Worth, Texas, here's six-year-old Tommy Jefferson, singing your favorite love songs." While experiencing stage fright.

* * *

Decades later, I have a dream. In a living room, a man has played a single note on a harmonica. I think, still in the dream, how a single note can transform into a chord, or rather a key, then a melody, then a song, then full instrumentation. The harmonica note somehow follows that thought and transforms into a song, and in the dream, I begin to sing……

I immediately awaken. Sixty-two years since I sang or even thought about those lyrics, yet they still break loose easily from their hiding place, as if setting the needle to a record pulled from a dusty collection. When I was six years old, that song was part of my repertoire—cute little Tommy Jefferson, singing the post-war torch songs of the day. Dressed in a bellhop uniform, I was the mascot on the Bobby Peters Jamboree, in the first days of live TV in Fort Worth.

It gets stranger. The song is with me as I get out of bed. I don't want to stop singing it just yet. The key from which it came in the dream is still firing its audible message, the neural pattern still glowing. I head straight to the piano to find the dream song key. B flat. When I look up the original sheet music from this 1954 Eddie Fisher hit, I see it was composed in—B flat.

*　*　*

WHAT STIMULATED THIS DREAM, THAT AWAKENS A FORgotten reality? Was it the three-year-old I was playing with the night before, somehow reminding me of myself? Why this song, "I Need You Now"? It is a plaintive song, the kind that has always resonated with me most deeply. I can sing a lonesome song with the best of them, at least to my ear. This is the key of my deepest emotions. The key *to* my deepest emotions. Vibrational, emotional memory. Lyrical memory. Tonal memory. The song of myself.

By age six, I had learned to sing of love and loss, and came to expect it. Love and loss. Loss and love. The minor keys have served as the undercurrents of my life. I've subsequently learned to play in a variety of keys, but the plaintive notes will always be there when love inevitably cycles to loss. I've learned to console myself with song. I know how soothing others can be, and how comforting one can be to others, with touch and sound.

*   *   *

I didn't choose show business as a career, although when I was five, I assumed it was not unusual to sing on live TV, have a fan club, and perform in and out of town. *"Tommy, will you sing Your Cheatin' Heart?" Cindy, 4th grade, Decatur, Texas,* the postcard said. Ah, to be loved by fourth graders when I wasn't even in school yet. Those girls in Decatur seemed to know something of love and loss, too, courtesy of Hank Williams. All my fan mail came from girls, a captive audience for pathos and its reverberations. Deep down there seemed to be understanding of the impermanence of love, and the chords it strikes.

Years later, I asked my father how I became a child performer. What started it all? My repertoire expanded to include piano, tap dancing, ventriloquism, and Victor Borge imitations. He said simply, "Ask your mother." It was the deepest conversation we ever had.

My mother was what would now be called a drama queen. She grew up the only child in a strict household with an absent father, another girl in a line of long-living matriarchs. The only family stories that were handed down dramatically emphasized the bravery, fortitude, and accomplishments of the women in the family. They brandished hot pokers at marauding soldiers during the Civil War while the men were out having their bravado turned into fear by war. Stories of the matriarchal fearlessness left to me to dig up the stories of the men in the family. Many of them were hard to track down.

Her dream was to be a dancer in New York City. Specifically, a Radio City Music Hall Rockette. Strict parenting, then the escape to marriage, then the war, relegated the dream to just a childhood fantasy. As a girl she was not allowed to dance or even go to school unchaperoned. She acted in school plays, and during WWII, had a job travelling with a partner on weekends to perform exhibition ballroom dancing, and teach dance. She was Miss Decatur, Texas, 1932.

One fateful afternoon, after the War, while making meat loaf and listening to the radio, she noticed her three-year-old singing along with the love songs of the day, then charmingly repeating the song and remembering the words. A star was born. I was given every opportunity to become the performer that lay dormant within her. She was back in show business.

My father knew all that, of course. He couldn't, or wouldn't say, "Tom, you were your mother's boy. You made her happy."

*　*　*

My first newspaper clipping, of course saved by my mother, was this: *A three-year-old will be the vocalist at a Tuesday recital at the home of Mrs. Edward Kirby. Tommy Jefferson, age three, will close the program with a song.* One of my first memories was being given a dollar to hold tightly in my hand to take to Mrs. Kirby's house, in the next block. Can you imagine sending a three-year-old down the street on his own these days with money for a singing lesson?

After my mother died, my sister and I were cleaning up her house. There were boxes and boxes of my newspaper clippings and photo shoots.......and nothing of my sister. We talked about it, and she cried. We have never been closer than that moment, that moment where I fully realized, sixty years later, that I got all the attention, and how hard it was for my sister to grow up in that situation. When you are getting all the attention, it is hard to see beyond that. Especially when you're a kid.

* * *

Mother's plan for my career in show business was flawed. I was an introvert; she was a stage mother. It seemed to me that she wasn't my real mother; she was my agent. I keep trying to remember being held, but it's just not there. My mother and father were supportive and well-meaning providers of food, shelter, and opportunity. They apparently loved my performing. But I don't remember nurture. To put a finer point to it, I missed out on the feeling of love and touch. I could only sing plaintive songs about love. I knew heartache, and sang it.

I believe my patterns of life started there. I was looking for love, I was singing of love, but I hadn't really experienced love, except through the lyrical narrative of song, a description of what love might be. From that time on, I wandered through life, looking for love.

* * *

In second grade, it was JoAnn Bailey. She was so beautiful, standing in front of me in the line to return from recess. I reached up on my tiptoes and kissed her. She seemed ok with it, and we went steady until the sixth grade, when she went off to Episcopal school.

I had found someone to love, and who I believed loved me. In those days, this meant trading wrist bracelets with the other's name inscribed on a disc. This was the 1950s elementary school version of getting tattooed with your loved one's name. The message was, move along, this person is taken. And, I've found love. It says so right here.

I vividly remember that day in the recess line. I didn't know JoAnn at that time, although I knew her name. It was her beauty that attracted me, specifically her face. I had to touch her face with my lips, to express not only my appreciation of her beauty, but to merge with it in some way, to become a part of it. There was no control over the urge. It was a numinous moment. It was love, finding its way outwardly, from within.

That would be the poetic interpretation, now described from afar. Alternatively, perhaps I was imprinted with songs of desire and need and was acting out the songs that I repeatedly performed to admiring adults. *I Need a Girl; Put Your Arms Around Me, Honey, Hold Me Tight; Secret Love; Wanted; Changing Partners; That's Amore…*the list goes on.

*   *   *

My signature song was…*Josephine*. I could easily wear the emotions of that song.

> *There never was a girl I could love*
> *Like I love my Josephine*
> *She's a flirt, she's a scamp, she's the vampiest vamp*
> *I've ever seen.*

It seems to me she's always flirting
With the fellas passing by
But when I say she winks then she tells me she thinks
There's a cinder in her eye.

I believe it would be better just to leave her and
forget her
Everybody says it would be wise
But each night when I go out to dance with
somebody else
I find myself dancing with tears in my eyes.

For there's nobody quite so nice
Who can be quite so mean
As my gal, what a gal,
Josephine

My six-year-old self naturally felt and expressed the emotional, lingering ritard while singing the line, *I find myself dancing with tears in my eyes.* Did I become drawn to JoAnn because I thought Josephine was magically appearing in the recess line? Or did the outpouring of love in the second grade prompt me, or rather my mother the agent, to add Josephine to my repertoire, so that when I sang it, I thought of JoAnn, and my emotions would be stirred to the angst required by the song?

That is one question I regret not asking my mother before she died.

* * *

Despite introversion and stage fright, I continued my performing career, but soon my enthusiasm began to wane. I came to realize I wasn't Ted Mack Amateur Hour or Mousketeer good at what I did; I was mostly just charming. This was another flaw in my mother's plan. When I realized I wasn't going to become a Mousketeer, I was extremely disappointed, as I wanted to meet and work with Annette. I cut an audition record for Lawrence Welk's Top Tunes and New Talent. The rejection letter from Santa Monica read simply, *We regret we are unable to place you on the program. If Mr. Welk is fortunate enough to continue to be successful on TV and if you keep improving, perhaps we can have the pleasure of hearing you again in the future.* Well, at least one of us made it. I still have that recording, and listening to it when I was much older, I agree with their assessment.

After I entered elementary school, I didn't like performing anymore. After all, I was performing for adults, not my school mates. My friends weren't so impressed by someone who could sing, play the piano, tap dance, and throw his voice to a wooden dummy. As a matter of fact, they likely thought that was quite odd. I began to think it odd also and became increasingly self-conscious, and, at one point, began to stutter.

I assume the stuttering was a transition to self-consciousness. At this point in my "career" my clear direction was to learn songs and sing them from memory, to please a mostly adult audience with my charm. With my real friends, rather than my audience, I was now required to come up with my own script, my own lyrics. This shift in expectations made me become fully, perhaps pathologically, self-conscious. I had no script, no original music. I was making the transition from child star to regular kid, and I found it rough going.

Years later, when I asked my mother about the short and self-limited period of stuttering, she told me this story. By the time I was a junior in high school, I was quite rebellious and hardly talked to my mother, father, sister, or brother. I kept to myself and my friends. When my mother and I did talk, as she tells the story, it was in a predictable fashion, that I now recall. She would sit in her living room chair, and I would stand beside it with my back to her, looking out the window into the street. We didn't face each other when we had serious talks. Ever the agent, she was leading a discussion in what career path I might follow after high school.

There were four careers my mother laid out for me. Doctor, lawyer, politician, preacher. Engineer had been on my list earlier in life, as my father was a civil engineer, a highwayman. At one time, I wanted to be like him. I was to find out my brain was not wired for engineering.

As my mother went over these options with me, she recalls I said I would be afraid to be a lawyer, because if I were in court, and had to plead a case, I might start stuttering. Stuttering seemed to be a subconscious fear, so much so, that I have no recollection of that conversation.

I once spoke with a therapist about these episodes. He asserted that stuttering was associated with anxiety, and as we began to discuss this theme of stuttering and self-consciousness......I began to stutter and became highly self-conscious of what I was saying. As if I were on stage under the bright lights with the monster with the large red eye closing in on me.

*　*　*

THANKFULLY, ALTHOUGH ANXIETY-PRODUCING PERFOR-mance was a big part of my life, there were idyllic times as well. In summertime I could run around barefoot, go to the river and fish and raft down the river, head off to the woods and hunt snakes and scorpions, and dream of being a cowboy. During the summer, day after day was the same breakfast, out the door to play all morning with my friends, back for lunch, then back out to play all afternoon, then dinner.

Two events brought dissonant chords to the idyll.

The first occurred on the fourth grade day when after school, I became absorbed in Charlie McFarland's oscilloscopes and radios, lost track of time, and got home very late for dinner. When I walked in and saw everyone already eating at the table, and the looks on their faces, I knew I was in big trouble. My mother, frantic, had called the police, as this was so unlike me.

Where have you been? Charlie McFarland's. *Who told you, you could go there?* Grandmother, I lied. Big mistake.

Grandmother was my mother's mother, who lived in a little house behind us. Part of the marriage agreement with my father, was that Grandmother had to live with us. She had divorced her husband in the 1930s for being a philanderer. Her divorce papers stated that he didn't come home on weekends, had a reputation around town, and wouldn't accompany her to church, causing others to talk. She always seemed very old and slow moving to me. She smiled rarely, and when she did, the smile was guarded. I couldn't stand to go into her house when she was boiling turnip greens or frying baloney. She kept her distance from the family, so we connected only for the rare babysitting episodes, which invariably included fried Vienna sausages, split down the middle to lie flat in the skillet, and a kitchen filled with grease vapor.

My mother stood up from the dining table, grabbed me by the arm, and marched me over to Grandmother's. There the relative I hardly knew took sides with her daughter over her grandson. I was caught in the lie. Then, my half-crazed mother took me to the bathroom, made me pull down my pants and underwear, and beat me with a belt while I leaned over the sink. It was the first and only whipping of my life, and it was a jim-dandy. I wonder now what was going through my father's mind. He was not involved in the punishment that was occurring just down the hallway.

I can remember leaning over the sink as if it were yesterday, her yelling about being late and lying as she whipped me. I also remember I didn't cry; I just stood there and took it. It was in some ways an out-of-body experience, as I don't really remember pain. I guess she thought she would beat me until I cried, and then I didn't. I wonder what made her stop? Then it was off to my room without supper.

I had never experienced such behavior before, and it changed things. My instinct was withdrawal, avoidance, mistrust. I was much more careful after that; it put a damper on my freedom. In my own mind, I had not done anything wrong to deserve such a beating. Except to lie. The cover-up was worse than the "crime." Nevertheless, that night changed my relationship with my mother permanently.

My mother brought up this incident as she was dying and told me she regretted it. So did I. That's ok, I probably said.

* * *

My father was responsible for the other major disillusionment of my childhood. He was unaware that it happened, and I never brought to his attention. It would have been too cruel to do that.

My father was a track star, having earned a scholarship to junior college for his speed and pole-vaulting skill. His medals were framed and proudly displayed in our house. One day, I asked him if he would show me how to get into the blocks for a sprint. He dug some holes in our front yard to get some traction, and we had a grand old time starting and racing across the yard.

My father was quite the competitor, in track, golf, chess, so much so that he never let me beat him, and quit playing chess with me when I began to win. In the front yard, with our crude starting blocks and subsequent sprints, he beat me every time. After all, I was probably nine years old.

Happy to have learned how to crouch and fire out, I took the digging tools back to our shed. As I returned to the back porch, I overheard my mother in the kitchen asking my father how it went. He fatefully said, "Well, he'll never amount to anything."

I wasn't supposed to hear that, and my father would have never said that if he knew I was listening, Surely he was saying it in a joking way. He was not a mean man. But I didn't know then that he was probably joking.

I sat on the back porch for a while, then picked up my baseball and played catch with myself, firing the ball at the steps and catching it on the rebound. Over and over, harder and harder. I loved baseball. I was done with track for a long time.

* * *

Love and loss. And hurt. I began to feel estranged from my parents. And yet, I remained the center of attention in the family, attention I no longer wanted.

Then, along came Bret.

Train of Thought

When I think about Bret,
I think of trains.
When I think about trains,
I think of Bret.

I remember the exact moment I learned I would have a younger sibling.

My father and I had just finished watching the Saturday Baseball Game of the Week with Dizzy Dean and Peewee Reese. We sat on the couch gazing at our Zenith black and white TV, eating chili dogs on TV tables. My father always laughed at Dizzy's Arkansas destruction of the English language (*"…he shoulda slud!…"*). It was a relief to see him laugh, as he often seemed so serious. That feeling of comfort led to a life of pleasurable baseball experiences for me. I felt comfortable with him in those moments, a closeness of shared interest and humor.

After the game, he announced that my sister and I were to gather in the living room with our mother, where they would tell us about something new that was coming. They invited us to guess what that might be.

A new car? Or TV? A dog? I wish I could watch that

moment on replay to hear all the guesses.

At some point when they tired of our queries, my mother informed us that she was pregnant. We were about to have a new member in our family!

Oh. I would have never guessed that. I remember feeling a little let down – after all, the surprise didn't seem to be for me. It was the same feeling I had when Grandmother Jefferson travelled to our house one Christmas morning with presents for us all. We had to wait hours for her to get there, but her present for me was gigantic, so I saved it for last. The culmination of my Christmas day was to open the box to find….an unpainted plaster of Paris wagon wheel. "Oh," I think I said, the only response I could muster. After she left, I asked my mother what I was supposed to do with it. She thought it should go on the wall. "Oh," I said. It did go on the wall for a while, then up to the attic, to be brought down on the rare occasions that my grandmother visited.

Learning I was to have a new brother or sister produced a much different kind of "oh." After all, this had never been discussed. We didn't have a family vote, just an announcement. I could sense that the dynamics of our family were about to change. Little did I, or for that matter any of us, know just how the trajectories of our lives would change.

The pregnancy was unplanned. My mother was forty-two, and my father fretted incessantly about money, as did most raised during the Depression. Our family of four was now to have a fifth mouth to feed, more clothes to buy, more room to provide. In my ten-year-old mind, I could practically see my father silently doing the math as he and my mother revealed our new, collective future. I could sense my mother's anxiety at having another pregnancy at her age. I remember leaving our family conference feeling a little confused, thinking I was supposed to be happy. I am pretty sure that after "oh," came "huh." It was just so surprising.

It was decided before he was born, that if he were a boy, his name was to be Bret, no middle name, named after Bret Maverick, a happy-go-lucky gambler and drifter from one of my father's favorite TV shows.

It turned out Bret was not so lucky. It was discovered soon after birth that he had Down Syndrome that left him functioning at a very low level for the forty-five years of his life. He was never able to talk or understand comprehensibly, making him quite challenging to communicate with. He observed others talking and tried to mimic conversation with wordless jabber. He did learn a few words, like "train", and his common manner of communication was to jabber-jabber-jabber as a lead up to the word, "TRAIN." This told us he was either thinking about trains, and he sensed that when he said "train" people would know what was on his mind; or he simply knew that saying "train" would get a positive response from us because he was actually saying a word.

His jabbering was constant, as he tried to communicate. We were like foreigners speaking a different language to each other without ever making progress in communication. This was particularly disruptive at the dinner table, where we were all used to discussing our days as a family. Bret's jabbering took over the dinner table, as we could not get a word in edgewise. If we began a conversation, Bret would want to be part of it, and dominate it with his jabbering. We really didn't know what to do. My father took to bringing a book to the table to read. I took to finishing my dinner quickly so that I could be excused, as the scene was too chaotic for me. It was off to my room to listen to baseball games on the radio. I began to feel alienated. It felt like I was living with aliens, and I couldn't shake the feeling. Up to this point in my life, it seemed as if I always knew what to do, or say. Now, I was stumped, and became self-conscious about it. I began to understand that the world didn't always go like you thought it might. As Bret found solace in trains, I found solace in baseball.

* * *

At our home in Fort Worth, my father built a train set on a 4x8 piece of plywood that folded up against the side of the garage. There was a big loop, a side track loop that went into a station, switches, painted paper mache mountains and lakes, additional side tracks to load cattle cars from vibrating corrals, and of course the engine itself, with a deeply satisfying transformer-powered whistle, and smoke coming out of the stack. I loved playing with that train. It was a work of art.

My father, a civil engineer, had grown up in Denison, Texas, a major train hub where three great railroads of the early 1900s met – the Missouri, Kansas, and Texas Railroads, known then as M-K-T, or Katy for short. His father had been a brakeman on the Frisco line. Being a brakeman was a dangerous job, because you had to jump from the top of one car to another to set the brakes.

My father never met his father. Family stories are hushed about what exactly transpired at the time of his birth, as there is no record his parents ever married or got divorced. My father's mother's parents died in their twenties, so she was raised by an aunt and uncle in central Texas. She grew to hate her uncle, who she said treated her like a slave. Although family members are a bit tight-lipped about what they know, my grandmother Myrtle was said as a teenager to have run away from home to be with her sister Fannie, who was being raised by a different aunt and uncle. Fannie lived near Denison, and in Texas in the early 1900s, if you ran away from home, you took the train. The next thing known about her is that she began living in Denison in the red-light district on Skiddy Street. Denison was known for being the major prostitution destination in north Texas for the railroad men from Missouri, Kansas, and Texas. One family rumor was that she became a hooker, a profession that would pay well for an orphaned runaway. My father was apparently the result of an accidental pregnancy and, with history repeating itself, was himself left in the care of his aunt and uncle (his father's brother and wife), until my grandmother made enough money to bring him to the rough railroad town at age four to help out with the boarding house she now ran. One of my father's cousins remembers my grandmother always dressing well and giving him fifty cents for meeting her at the train station and escorting her to their house when she visited.

I liked my Grandmother Jefferson, and when I was a kid, I spent a week at her home in Denison for a few summers in a row. Her husband Acie owned a small grocery store and let me slice baloney, read comic books, drink all the Choc-o-loc I wanted, and shoot BB guns at egg crate targets with cardboard backing to save the BBs for reuse. He had a habit of chewing tobacco which included bringing his spittoon to the dinner table. I was mesmerized when he would smush cornbread into his milk glass, then eat it with a spoon. I'm pretty sure Acie's habits are why we rarely visited as a family, but I liked him, and was sad when he killed himself one Christmas Day.

Grandmother Jefferson was a cheery woman, and my summer trips to Denison always culminated in a trip to Lake Texoma on the Texas-Oklahoma border, to fish for sand bass. She taught me how to fish, and how to drink beer – ice-cold cans of Busch Bavarian, ornamented with snowy peaks and dark blue sky, perfect for the hot summertime Texas weather. That evening, her sister Fannie would fry the sand bass for a huge meal in celebration of the day's catch, and the end of the vacation. I have nothing but fond memories of those days in Denison with Myrtle, Acie, Fannie, and her husband Bennett.

∗ ∗ ∗

THUS TRAINS WERE AN IMPORTANT PART OF MY FATHER'S upbringing – his father was a brakeman, his mother found her place in the train world, he was raised near the railroad, he had built an elaborate trainset in the garage that we both enjoyed, …and he became an engineer, albeit a civil engineer. When my brother was born and there were limited ways of connecting with him, my father built a train set for him in his bedroom. Bret played with it constantly; he never tired of watching the train go round and round, mesmerized. He had a record player to play train songs; he loved to imitate the whistles. He could remain occupied for hours, in some other world. We were all glad he had something to be interested in, as it gave us some relief from the sense of unsettlement in our family. It was reassuring to hear the train whistles coming from his bedroom. Bret lived in his train world in the evenings while the rest of us watched TV.

My first year in college I lived in a dorm, where we were assigned roommates. In the room next to me lived a very quiet and strange boy, who spent hours in his room reading about trains and poring over train schedules. His roommate, a New Jersey street boy, left college after the first semester because he couldn't fathom or communicate with his roommate. I knew what he was going through. The New Jersey kid, I mean.

I suppose trains, like any other interest or hobby, can become an obsession. I'm obsessed with trying to figure out why people get obsessed about such things. I never took up the fascination with trains, but I know that there are those who do. But if it weren't for trains, I wouldn't be telling this story.

Trains. Baseball. Brothers. Fathers. Family secrets. Obsessions. Hookers. Trains.

*　*　*

IN HONOR OF MY GRANDMOTHER, AND THE THEME OF trains in my life, I wrote this poem.

The Frisco Line

Grandma was a hooker
Or so the legend goes
She plied her trade in Texas
A hundred years ago

She couldn't stand Odessa
Her uncle wasn't kind
The way out was a ticket
On the Katy Frisco Line.

Her sister lived in Greenwood
The train was their connection
So Grandma rode, she ran away

To seek a new direction.

She met a brakeman on the line
His home was the caboose
He knew the ways to slow a train
and let his juices loose

They slept with fate on that cruel date
In April 1912
She did not see the iceberg sea
Into which she would delve

So when she looked up to the stars
Lying on the ground
She did not know, but soon found out
Titanic had gone down.

Well that's not good her sister said
But decisions had been made
Then all too soon her Georgie boy
Sprang from the tracks she'd laid.

She soon found out to her dismay
A brakeman has no home
He rides the rails and spreads his sails
His true love is to roam

She did learn from the railroad
That boom towns were the key
Lots of men and money
Waiting to be freed.

She left her boy with next of kin
And went on up the line
To Skiddy Street where the railroads meet

And hooking was not a crime.

What a life she told herself
The money's pretty good
I'm doing this for Georgie boy
And Texas motherhood

Soon she had a boarding house
And needed help to tend
So then she sent for Georgie
And tried to make amends

She taught me how to sit by the lake
And drink an ice-cold beer
Then go home for some fried sand bass
There was nothing there to fear

So life is one long story
It's not just one lifetime
History's soon forgotten
As it fades into time.

This story keeps on going
I'm here to say I'm fine
With the life born on the Texas plains
A tale of the Frisco line.

Becoming an M.D.

I am often asked why I wanted to go to medical school, or when I first knew I wanted to be a doctor, or how I chose Family Practice. In truth, it seemed like medical school chose me, then told me what I was to be.

My first career turning point hinged on saying no to mice, at the end of my second year at University of Virginia, when I needed to declare a major. I was interested in what made living things tick and narrowed the decision to psychology or biology. At that time, psychology was in the B.F. Skinner phase of learning how to predict human behavior from the performance of mice in a maze, and I wasn't too keen on studying mice or rats in mazes. So biology it was. It wouldn't be the last time I said no to matters of the mind, although my interest rose considerably later in life, when my thoughts turned to the nature of thought and its disorders.

Biology led me to the most interesting and challenging class of my life. I had not been that interested in most school topics, until I took Molecular Biology of the Gene. DNA had recently been discovered to hold a secret code to life, and the class opened me up to a new world, one that existed at a microscopic level beyond what could be sensed with the unaided eye. The complexity of cells, and how they aggregate into larger beings and communicate with each other, was fascinating to me, and still is. There was an invisible world, beyond complete comprehension, that held the secrets of life. I would be an explorer. Every pathway provided more questions. I wasn't thinking of a career, I was immersed in the passion of discovery.

Many of the students in Molecular Biology already planned to apply to medical school. Why not apply, I thought, as I was not sure at the time where else my interests would lead. It would be an opportunity to further explore the mysteries of living things. To my surprise, I was accepted at U. Va. I was going to medical school, not because I wanted to be a doctor, but because my life just flowed in that direction. I have no idea where I would be now, or what I would be doing, if I had not been accepted to medical school.

The next twist in life was literally pulled out of a hat. On December 1, 1969, two months into medical school, several of us med students sat in a room listening to numbers being called over the radio. Student deferments to the draft were no longer a possibility – if your number was called, you enlisted, no matter what you were doing. The lottery was based on birthdate, and it was known beforehand that if you were in the first 150 or so selected, your fate was in the hands of the US government and its figurehead, Richard Nixon, whom I deeply despised. My number was 300. I was free to continue with medical school.

*　*　*

THE FIRST YEAR AND HALF OF MEDICAL SCHOOL WAS brutal. It was all classroom work – anatomy, physiology, embryology and the like, with classes from eight-to-five weekdays and eight-to-twelve on Saturday. With that schedule, and little time for study, I quickly figured the only way to survive was to pay close attention in class, take copious notes, and review my notes before exams. I had long ago mastered the art of figuring out what was going to be on tests and focusing there. I was good at tests.

The first test was in lab. Lab was where we learned about the components of blood, urine, and other bodily samples, and how that testing was used for diagnosis. The anxiety level before that test was incredible, as no one knew what to expect, and it seemed more of a test to determine whether you had it in you to continue. After two months of living with med students from all over the country, I was not sure I was in the right place. I made up my mind that if I failed this test, I would leave medical school, and go on to something else. I suspect others thought the same.

There were fifty stations in the lab, set up with microscopes or pictures of various cellular pathology. With a minute at each station, we had to identify what we were looking at, and its significance. Thanks to my good visual memory, this test turned out to be easy for me, and I did well. Maybe med school wasn't going to be so hard after all.

*　*　*

Our class was exactly 100 students, ninety-eight men and two women. Classes were held in amphitheaters, just enough seats for the entire class, so we were stuffed in, day after day, all taking the same courses. There were those who sat up front, and those who sat in the back. I was a back-pew person. From there I could survey the entire room, where it was easier to trade whispered wisecracks with my back-of-the-class cronies. The few dropouts came from the back of the class, those of us watching from the periphery, ready to bolt at a moment's notice.

The lecture classes were peppered with various labs, which allowed much more freedom to explore, and, quite literally, cut up. I am positive that everyone in our class had the most vivid memories of anatomy lab.

There were four of us to a corpse, the Jane and John Does of the day. The room reeked of formaldehyde, not a pleasant smell. But there we learned what organs, muscles, nerves, blood vessels, and brains looked like when not covered by skin and bone. Dark humor abounded, as future doctors cut skin slabs to make masks, with eye, nose, and mouth holes.

But most of the first year and a half of med school was classroom work, grinding through rote learning, not that much different from K-twelve and four years of college. There was just more of it, and everything was important. We were desperate to get on with the task of putting our knowledge into the practice of diagnosing and treating real people. That is where we would learn to be doctors. When we transitioned from the classroom to seeing patients in the hospital under supervision, it was known as heading to "the floor."

Every day on the floor provided a learning experience, as we rotated through different services. Besides providing experience in all disciplines, this was the beginning, for those who were uncommitted like me, to find out where we might best be suited as doctors. Many had their minds made up before they came to medical school, but not me. I had no idea. Where would the flow take me now?

* * *

MY FIRST SIX-WEEK ASSIGNMENT WAS THE PSYCHIATRIC ward, and it was with great excitement that I showed up for rounds at 0700 that first Monday morning. I was whisked with others into a small room, where aides were preparing an older woman for electroshock therapy. I was horrified to find that my first exposure to treating real patients involved putting paddles on a woman's head and sending a current through her that stiffened and arched her entire body, which then came to rest in a senseless, limp daze.

I was determined, after she recovered, to learn her perspective. She was in her sixties, severely depressed, very slow in movement and speech, and received shocks three times a week. I asked her if the shocks were helping her. Her reply? "I guess so." I guessed not, but I wasn't in charge.

Day two was the once-a-week chairman rounds, where the chairman of the department oversaw a meeting of all the house staff, interns, residents, and students. We all crowded into a conference room and seated ourselves around a table that could fit the twenty-five or so of us who were there, as the residents presented cases, or follow-ups from the floor for discussion.

At that first meeting, I got another perspective of 1970s psychiatry in Virginia. We gathered at the conference table at exactly 0800, waiting for the head of the department to make his grand entrance. And grand it was. Through a door only available to him, a small man with a Freud beard and long white coat majestically entered, taking his place at the head of the table as the room quickly silenced. Following him into the room, incredibly, were two black servants, a man who held his chair for him and positioned it while he sat, the other a woman carrying a silver tea set on a platter placed for his sipping pleasure during the presentations. It was immediately clear who the boss was, and we could only aspire to graduate from drinking bad coffee from our lowly Styrofoam cups. By this second day on the floor, I already knew that this would be my last psychiatry rotation.

But I was scheduled to be there for six weeks and had to make the best of it. We were all required to follow one patient on the ward for an in-depth analysis, which we would write up. I was astonished to find that there was someone I was familiar with on the floor.

Don was the 6'10" starting center of the UVa basketball team. College basketball is huge in that part of the world, and although at the time the team was not in the upper echelons of the sport, we nevertheless got to watch national championship teams from Duke and North Carolina when they came to Charlottesville. Those were games that literally everyone showed up for, including me, so I was familiar with the team.

Don was the star of the team, not quite good enough to have been selected by the top teams in the country but was quite the recruiting coup for Virginia. Essentially every play involved him shooting, passing or defending. He was the star of a not-so-great team, playing on a big stage.

His play began to be erratic, and in the middle of one game late in his second season he seemed confused, dribbled the ball to the sidelines, and was done for the season. No one really knew what the problem was. There were stories of an injury, and it was announced that he would not be returning to the team for the rest of the year.

Now, here he was, in a room on the psych ward, and I picked Don for my required in-depth assessment. For whatever reason, most likely because I was truly trying to understand him rather than approaching him as a "case" to be "cured," we took to each other right away. He had suffered a schizophrenic break, at a time when that most commonly and unfortunately occurs, around twenty years of age. I had heard and read enough about schizophrenia to know that it was thought at the time to be a disorder of purely psychological origin. The predominant theory was that it was due to an overly demanding mother putting a child into double binds, resulting in the child facing the constant dilemma of being unable to resolve conflicts, or escape them. The voices heard were Mother's voice, transformed and in control.

To me, Don seemed perfectly normal, though he struggled with being unable to sort out the various voices he heard. We all have a running thread of thought, and talk to ourselves silently, or sometimes out loud, and even internally articulate the pros and cons when a decision has to be made. Don couldn't sort out which voice to listen to, leaving him helpless, confused, and frightened.

That did not prevent us from having great conversations. When his mind was distracted into following a train of thought or dialog, the voices fell silent, as he was using his own. It was only when left to his own thoughts, that his life became confusing.

We were a great Mutt and Jeff. Don was 6'10", I was 5'10". For six weeks we chatted three times weekly. Because it was noticed by others that we got along well, he was allowed out of the locked facility, only with me, to take walks around the campus, and even visit his apartment. We had a great time, and quite honestly, it didn't seem to me that there was anything wrong with him, except being troubled by this affliction that no one really had an answer for.

Because we became such good friends, as I was nearing the end of the six-week rotation, I was pulled aside and told that I needed to tell Don that I would be leaving soon, going on to my next rotation, and wouldn't be around anymore. I was not to see him again, as I was told part of his therapy was to develop skills for, or get used to, obstacles in life, such as the loss of friendships, or professional help.

I was shocked to hear this but did what I was told. I sat down with him, and uncomfortably told him I wouldn't be seeing him anymore. I said that I had really enjoyed our time together and wished him the best of luck. He was confused, angry, and sad. I fought back the tears but stuck to what I was told I needed to do. I felt awful about it.

But not as awful as when I found out, a few months later, that Don had killed himself while out on a pass.

* * *

It was inconceivable to me that schizophrenia was simply the result of a demanding mother. After all, I had a demanding mother, and while it had other effects, schizophrenia wasn't one of them. At that time there were alternate theories. One of the more controversial and renegade psychiatrists of the time was R.D. Laing. His book, *The Divided Self*, was quite popular in the lay literature, as it challenged the paradigm of the day. Labelled as anti-psychiatry, against electroshock therapy and powerful sedating medication as treatment, Laing fit in perfectly with my anti-authoritarianism. His theory was later proven to be wrong, but he did advance the idea that the behavior of individuals with psychosis was a not due to a "break" with reality, but searching for how best to deal with the unfortunate and valid reality they were faced with. This was in keeping with what I had observed with Don.

At the end of our rotation, we were required to write an essay on an aspect of psychiatry of our choice. I chose to write a review of *The Divided Self* and described how I found some of Laing's thinking to be valid, in my limited experience with schizophrenia.

The papers were graded by the notorious head of the department. When I got mine back, there was an "F" in red ink on the front page, with the comment, "R.D. Laing is out of the mainstream of modern psychiatry." There were no other remarks on the essay.

I didn't think anything of it. After all, I had my opinion about schizophrenia, the head of the department had his. I couldn't imagine that a person who went out of his way to look like Freud, and had slaves tending to him, was exactly a progressive thinker.

But I found that by getting an F on the paper, I was being failed in the rotation, which meant I would have to take the six weeks over again. This required a trip to the Dean of the Medical School. What a start to patient care: my first experience with real patients, and I was already in the Dean's office, for the crime of thinking out of the box, of bucking tradition.

I didn't back down. I explained that I went to every conference I was supposed to, did all my work, missed no days, worked hard, had successfully engaged a schizophrenic patient, and provided what I thought to be a beneficial connection in his life. I did not understand what writing a paper challenging the psychiatric paradigm had to do with patient care. So what if R.D. Laing was not considered to be mainstream? What could that possibly have to do with my education? What would I learn by taking the rotation over? Was I as a future physician supposed to accept everything I was taught as true, when it was clear that no one understood the cause of schizophrenia, including the head of the department?

My argument worked. The Dean agreed with me and intervened to pass me on to the next rotation. But I now knew that psychiatry was not the field for me. Between witnessing electroshock therapy, having to intentionally disappoint a vulnerable psychiatric patient, and being failed for challenging the paradigm, I found the methods of psychiatry to be crude and inhumane.

It went on like that. Surgery rotation – the head of the department was a gruff man who threw instruments in the operating room. Pediatrics? The doctors were great, but I couldn't see spending a good portion of my life specializing in babies with ear infections, especially after six weeks in the Pediatric Night Clinic. OB-GYN was a disaster. Never having seen the pain and intensity of childbirth, the experience left me bug-eyed and speechless. I witnessed one of the residents, in responding to the cries of a woman in delivery, literally slap her to get her to quiet down. It didn't seem like I needed to learn that.

✳ ✳ ✳

BY MY THIRD YEAR, IT WAS CLEAR I WAS CUT OUT FOR general practice. I had a distant relative who was a country doctor in Piney River, Virginia, and my mother arranged a visit to him near the end of college. His office was in his residence in the woods, and he often traded services for hams and tobacco. In the evenings, he played boogie-woogie piano. Now that's the life, I thought. Piney River Smith, they called him. I could do that.

And so I signed up for a three-month rotation in Buckingham County, Virginia, the poorest county in the state. The medical school had set up a clinic in trailers, providing the only available medical care to the county's predominantly black population. I was taken by local community health specialists to visit those too infirm to travel. This was my first exposure to the living situation of the rural black American poor.

I visited a woman in her nineties, too frail to move, to determine if there was anything that could be done to help her. She was lying on a bare mattress on the top bed of a four-tier sleeping bunk in the corner, and had not moved for quite some time. The house consisted of one large room divided into two areas, a living/sleeping area and a kitchen, housing a family of ten. A large turnip patch provided staples. She was near the end of a long life, and there was nothing I could offer other than changing her position to avoid bedsores. The health aides knew that; the real purpose of my visit was for me to see the environment the clinic population lived in.

The rural poor of Buckingham County were grateful to have doctors come and visit, even if they were medical students. I learned how much a positive attitude can overcome having nothing. Later in life, I would have local Eugene patients who griped about being poor. I bit my tongue; if only they knew.

My experience in Buckingham County supported my intuition that this was what I wanted to do: engage with people who were in real need and who were thankful you were there, suggest a course of action using the tools at hand and based on what could realistically be done, and help people make medical decisions, often life or death decisions. What a gift, to be allowed to do that!

So that is how I decided to go into general practice, as it was called then. It started with a passionate interest in biology, the study of living things. Now I would study humans, cradle to grave, and try to help.

But there were more twists of fate along the path.

Clarence

⸻

Clarence was a fifty-five-year-old black man from a remote area in Virginia, who was admitted to the neurology ward because he was confused and unintelligible. Protocol called for the medical student to see new hospital admissions first, followed by house staff evaluation. As it turned out, in this first responsibility as a medical student on the medical floor, I was the only person who had an actual "conversation" with Clarence before he began to deteriorate.

I sat down in a chair next to the hospital bed, and observed a thin, anxious man with a wild look in his eyes. "What's wrong?" I asked. Understanding my question, he connected eye to eye with me and tried to say something, but only guttural sounds came out, the sounds one makes when trying to cry for help in a paralysis dream. He looked at me frantically and pointed to his mouth. As I was about to ask my next question, he lapsed into a startled incoherence, as if he had lost touch with where he was, and who I was. I looked in his mouth carefully and saw only that he had many teeth missing. With conversation no longer possible, I examined the rest of him thoroughly, but found no clues to the cause of his confusion. He lived alone, and I was told friends had found him like this. They had no further information to offer, as he kept to himself. He did not appear to be going downhill quickly, but his diagnosis wasn't obvious. After completing my examination, I reported immediately up the chain of command to the supervising resident physician and dutifully entered my handwritten findings in the nurse's note section of the hospital chart reserved for medical students.

The resident reviewed my history and findings, examined Clarence, and likewise found no reason for his confusion. His vital signs were stable, so he was not at risk of death, allowing the puzzle to be solved urgently but methodically. Clarence was to become that most prized finding in a university medical school and teaching hospital—the medical mystery.

The first guess was subdural hematoma – that he had fallen, hit his head, and bled into his brain. After CT scan and Xrays of his head had ruled out traumatic or structural abnormalities of his brain and skull, he underwent the medical workup of the unknown, starting with increasingly more detailed blood tests and toxicologies. When the initial blood tests came back, we had our first clue: hypercalcemia – his blood calcium was very high. This was the explanation for his confusion, as the brain doesn't work properly with high calcium levels. But what was causing the hypercalcemia?

The second most prized medical school case study was a medical mystery presenting with hypercalcemia. There was no better teaching case. Why? The differential diagnosis, or list of conditions that can cause hypercalcemia, is long. All possibilities needed to be explored, and all possible conditions had to be ruled out. Clarence was to get the million-dollar workup.

The most common causes of hypercalcemia are hyper-parathyroidism (an overactive parathyroid gland), or an occult malignancy or cancer. Virtually any type of cancer can cause hypercalcemia, so that did not narrow it down. Less common were several hormonal or drug-induced disorders, followed by a list of much rarer causes. We were taught to start with the most likely diagnosis and work our way through all possibilities, until we discovered the cause, the final diagnosis. In the late 1960s it could take days to get test results back, so the initial next steps were to start the endocrine tests, with its barrage of blood and urine tests, while proceeding with the workup for occult malignancy – upper and lower GI tests, small intestinal tests, liver and kidney tests, bone scans. No organ was to be left out of the investigation. These were the days before endoscopes and MRIs, so many of the tests involved use of barium or other contrast agents, and Xrays that required specific prepara-tions that could interfere with other testing. All of these took time to coordinate, schedule, interpret, discuss, and often repeat if questionable.

Complicating the workup was that practically every spe-cialty service was consulted. Every specialist brought their own attending doctors, medical students, interns, residents, and suggestions. Neurologists, gastroenterologists, oncolo-gists, endocrinologists, hematologists, and pulmonologists began to parade through Clarence's room. Each specialty service had its own recommended set of tests, and schedul-ing and coordinating the tests and specialty visits became a logistical challenge. In the extremely competitive atmo-sphere of a modern medical school, each specialty team was either confident that they would be the first to come up with the diagnosis, or emphatically convinced that the cause of Clarence's illness was unrelated to their specialty area. Medical mysteries produced the specialist merry-go-round. Generally, if you were the object of a merry-go-round, you are by definition in trouble—it is diagnostic of uncertainty.

Test after test came up negative, and though his blood calcium was treated (via another complicated and often unsuccessful set of procedures that nevertheless provided a teaching opportunity), Clarence remained unresponsive. His heart was in good condition, his breathing not a problem, but his mind was not there. He could put up no objection to the swirl while his body was scoured to find the cause of his demise, and it was becoming increasingly clear that Clarence might not leave the hospital alive.

Weeks passed. As a lowly medical student, I became an observer as the higher ups took charge of the care. Specialty after specialty, and test after test, failed to come up with an answer. You cannot imagine how frustrating it is when the collective brainpower of an entire modern medical school is unable to come up with a diagnosis. The doctors would not give up until Clarence died, and then they still would not give up until his body was autopsied, that final solemnity with knives and bone saws that would reveal the pathology that had escaped their slightly less invasive probing. The autopsy, a patient's final exam, was often performed before a gallery of medical students eating their sandwiches, as there were no lunch breaks in medical school.

I left before a conclusion was reached, as my time on that service had ended, and I moved to a different part of the hospital for my next rotation. There I was presented with a new barrage of people to interview, examine, evaluate, and work up. I was somewhat relieved that Clarence was oblivious to his testing, yet I was unsettled by the way he had been reduced to an experimental animal, something I had been exposed to, and never felt good about. Although I understood the need for the sacrifice of a few to help the many, accepting the need for sacrifice required emotional detachment. A physician's emotional aloofness starts in medical school. It is part of the training. And so, I managed to forget about Clarence.

*　*　*

Several months later, one of the residents informed me that I needed to be sure to come to the next CPC, the Clinical Pathological Conference. The CPCs were hour-long monthly meetings where interesting and challenging cases, the real puzzlers, were presented and discussed during the lunch hour. A pathological conference meant that the diagnosis had been made, that there were pathology slides, or an autopsy, that would reveal the culprit, in this case, the murderer. The medical mystery was presented by residents in a who-done-it fashion to a panel of experts, where the story and evidence were reviewed in a step-by-step fashion. There would be pauses at given points in the evaluation to allow discussion of what you should be thinking at this point, and what next steps you would take. The conference was open to all doctors and medical students. CPCs were one of the most interesting and stimulating conferences in medical school, attended by most med students, residents, and importantly, the teaching physicians, who did not like to be stumped in front of their peers and students. The conferences took place in the largest auditorium in the school, which would be packed with a sea of white-coated doctors and students armed with take-out lunches and strong coffee, anxious to learn, to see if you could come up with the diagnosis, and then be praised for your acumen. Only the most puzzling cases were presented. You did not want to miss the CPC. The hospital had to turn down the air conditioning to compensate for the aggregate body heat and sizzling brains.

I was told I had to be there, as it was Clarence who was to be discussed. They had finally found the answer, and it turned out that I was the one who had unknowingly left the definitive clue that had been overlooked.

As Clarence deteriorated, it became clear that an occult cancer was consuming him, but the million-dollar workup had not identified the primary cause. As he began to show evidence of metastasis, those areas were biopsied, but that still did not reveal the source organ. Tests were repeated to no avail. As the case and the workup was presented at the CPC, not one doctor out of the hundreds in the room guessed the answer. This demonstrated the true meaning of occult malignancy. Discovering the source of Clarence's cancer had stumped the entire staff of one of the top medical schools in the country.

It was then revealed how the diagnosis had been made. After every conceivable test revealed nothing, a compulsive resident decided to review all the paperwork from the beginning, to start from scratch, to see if anything had been missed. He started with my very first handwritten chart note, where I had documented that in Clarence's last conscious moment, he opened his mouth and pointed to his throat. Clarence had likely been seen by fifty doctors, the best of the best, all of whom had looked in his mouth, scrupulously looking for anything, and finding nothing. But the resident was intrigued that my notes might indicate where Clarence's problem was. One specialty area that had not been consulted was the ENT

(Ear Nose Throat) service, often forgotten in the specialist merry-go-round. After all, the best of the best doctors had already carefully examined Clarence's oral cavity.

The head of the ENT department and his students were asked to examine him. He was the first to actually stick his fingers down Clarence's throat, because that is what ENT docs do as part of their complete exam. And there, at the very base of his tongue, hidden from sight of all test modalities, was the unmistakable nodularity of a cancer of the base of the tongue. He couldn't see it, but he could feel it. The only way to diagnose Clarence's cancer, in those pre-endoscopic days, would have been to stick your fingers down his throat to feel the far reaches of the tongue hidden from sight. This was not part of a standard exam taught to future doctors, as such an exam required anesthesia or a comatose patient, to prevent the patient from gagging, or biting the physician. Human bites are some of the worst to treat, the mouth hiding vast hordes of unpleasant, invasive, and occasionally lethal bacteria, so much care must be taken when you stick your fingers in someone's mouth. But there was no way to diagnose Clarence without doing exactly that. This simple diagnostic maneuver, requiring no fancy equipment, had not been performed.

As it turned out, the mystery was solved only days before Clarence's death. Thankfully, it would not have made any difference if the cancer had been found earlier, for at the time, that type of cancer was not curable, and led to an unpleasant death in a short period of time, which is literally what we were observing. He was a dead man when he hit the door of the hospital, and was fortunate the hypercalcemia and confusion rendered him unaware of the subsequent extensive and invasive workup.

The presentation was made to the entire school for two reasons. One was a chance to review the workup of a mystery condition with only hypercalcemia and confusion as the initial clue. The other was that specialists should consider reading the medical student's notes. Significantly, the medical student's notes were handwritten; every other doctor produced a dictated assessment. Clarence had pointed to his problem; it was right there in my notes. The medical student wasn't expected to make the diagnosis. After all, it had just been shown that an entire medical school staff couldn't make the diagnosis. Medical student notes were rarely looked at, because they were handwritten, and included in the nurses' section of the chart, hidden from view of the chart tab reserved for the typed, and easier to read house-staff and attending dictations. As the hordes of specialists descended on Clarence, they only reviewed each other's notes, and my findings disappeared from the typed record. And there, in my notes, when I asked Clarence what was wrong, he had looked at me wildly and pointed to what I now realized was his tongue, the source of his problem.

They still present Clarence's case every now and then at U.Va., as it is a great teaching case on many levels. I learned that no detail was too small, and that the answer to a complicated problem could be right there in front of you, within the touch of your fingertips. But you had to pay close enough attention, review all the evidence, and perform a careful exam.

I was memorialized as a beginning medical student, who knew very little at that point. But I could describe what I saw and heard, and I did. My reporting was overlooked. As compulsive as the teaching staff had been in their thorough and expensive testing, only one resident had been compulsive enough to read the lowly medical student's notes.

Those were the points that were driven home at the CPC, for the entire medical school to hear. I had an additional takeaway. For the rest of my career, I could easily recall Clarence, with the wild look in his eyes, pointing to himself, as a reminder to listen and observe carefully, and follow up on any clues.

Westward Ho

Irene, good night
Irene, good night.
Goodnight Irene, goodnight Irene
I'll see you in my dreams.

Sometimes I live in the country.
Sometimes I live in town.
Sometimes I have a great notion,
To jump in the river and drown.

It was 1972. Medical school was drawing to a close; I would soon be an MD. What was next? Where would I continue my education?

Every year, fourth year medical students visit graduate medical programs around the country, looking for the right place to continue their education. After the interviews, the students, and the programs, both enter their prioritized choices into a national database, through which students and schools are matched. The momentous day when medical students find out where they will live and work for at least the next year is known as Match Day. Match Day is a turning point in every medical student's life. You don't necessarily get your top choice; fate plays a role.

I finished high school in Alexandria, Virginia, and had lived in Charlottesville for eight years during college and medical school. I needed a change. Typically, Virginia graduates applied to other institutions in the South – Duke, North Carolina, Vanderbilt, Emory. I loved Virginia but wanted to live in a different part of the United States—somewhere other than a Southern school. But where?

I made up my mind one summer weekend before my last year in medical school. Three years earlier, several of us had rented a place outside of Charlottesville, a ramshackle three-bedroom, two-story house with a kitchen, living room, and bathroom, on several acres of secluded property. The house had been scheduled to be demolished, but my medical school friend Ty convinced the owner to rent it to us for $100/month. To reduce our monthly obligation, we squeezed in as many people as possible. Ultimately, six of us lived there for three years with Beulah, our sweet dog–three of us in single bedrooms, a couple who slept by the oil furnace in the dirt basement, and a sixth who lived in a dirt dugout cubby-hole on the side of the house. We were three medical students, two college grads doing odd jobs, and an itinerant cook who had most recently worked at the Tassajara Bakery. It seemed exotic to live with someone who had just come from from California, but as it turned out, our menu was usually rice and vegetables, lentils, and bread. It was boring fare, but cheap; and cheap was the reason we were all there.

On the weekend I made my decision, everyone was gone except for Beulah and me, and I was not working or on call. I was looking forward to the solitary peace and quiet of sitting on the front porch and reading. I had been saving

Ken Kesey's *Sometimes a Great Notion* for just such an occasion, and immediately became engaged in a novel so epic that I couldn't put it down. I finished it in one continuous read, interrupted only by eating, sleeping, resting my eyes, and daydreaming myself into the novel.

I was entranced with Kesey's story of the Stampers and the descriptions of the logging, relentless rain, and flooding rivers of Oregon. I'll never forget the climax of the novel, with Hank Stamper rafting down the river with his brother Henry's severed arm attached to a pole, giving the finger salute to passersby. Oregon seemed an exciting place to live. I had to see it for myself. If it was good enough for Ken Kesey, one of my cultural heroes, it was good enough for me. A medical internship in Oregon was just the vehicle to get there.

Les, another medical student in the house, was headed to Seattle to apply to the internal medicine program at University of Washington. His brother Ralph had just opened a law practice there and spoke of the city glowingly. With the Vietnam War ongoing and its outcome unsure, we had lost faith in our own government and considered Canada as an alternative place to live and work, so a plan emerged. We would drive from Charlottesville to Montreal, visit and apply at McGill University's graduate medical program, then take the trans-Canadian railway to Vancouver, British Columbia's Vancouver General Hospital and Health Sciences Center. From there we would travel to Seattle, interview at the University of Washington Medical Center, then on to Oregon Health Sciences University in Portland. If we had time, we would also visit UCSF Medical Center in San Francisco.

Although we arranged appointments in Seattle and Portland, we decided to simply show up at McGill and

Vancouver General. We were confident we could breeze in, impress our future employers as graduates of one of the best medical schools in the country, get accepted every-where we applied, and simply prioritize our list. What could go wrong?

As it turned out, plenty. For starters, we didn't look the part of aspiring physicians. Les had long black hair and a bushy, scraggly beard. I had shoulder-length hair and wire rims, my hair pony-tailed for presentation purposes. We wore Levi's and sandals. We didn't judge people by their looks, why should they? We set off from Charlottesville in my '68 VW Bug in the fall of '72.

* * *

We arrived in Montreal in the afternoon, walked to the McGill administrative offices, and explained that we were American medical students wishing to apply for an internship or residency. The woman eyeballed our scruffiness and said, politely but resolutely, "We're not taking American medical students." We had driven 700 miles and twelve hours to receive a one-sentence rejection by the first person we talked to. We snuck a glance at each other, exchanging a silent but understood "oops." Scratch McGill off the list. We asked if we could at least stay the night, perhaps in the interns' quarters, so that we might get cleaned up before our trans-Canadian railway adventure. The friendly woman agreed and showed us to our quarters for the night. It occurred to us that she had no way of knowing that we were medical students, as we never got around to filling out an application, but it was a good line. If push ever came to shove, we could always secure a room for the night by going to a teaching hospital and saying we were medical students looking for a job. That might come in handy in the future.

The next morning, it was off to the railroad station. It would take us seventy-one hours to travel the 2,300 railway miles from Montreal to Vancouver B.C. We purchased the cheapest seats, which meant no sleeping berth. Sitting and sleeping in a seat for over three days seemed doable, especially given they were window seats. It was exciting to pull slowly out of Montreal and head west. From the window of the rail car, Canada soon turned into mostly empty land, with the passing terrain allowing unfocused reflection and napping. I let my thoughts go and drifted off to sleep.

I was awakened by the train slowing down. We were north of the Great Lakes; the wind was blowing snow at a forty-five-degree angle, and there an incongruously dark and ominous white-out stretched as far as I could see. Then, out of the snow appeared a native, dressed in bulky furs. Behind her was what seemed to be a station house, but visibility was so limited it was not clear if there was even a town. The passenger boarded, in the middle of nowhere, in a blizzard. It was entirely possible that she had simply flagged the train down, and the friendly Canadian engineer stopped to extricate her from the snowstorm. Perhaps that is how things are done in Canada – just wander out to the tracks and wave down a passing train.

As the train re-accelerated, I was reminded of the story I had just read in the Mark Twain compendium I had brought—the deliciously wicked 1868 tale *Cannibalism in the Car*. Twain spins a yarn of a group of Congressmen heading west by train out of Chicago. The train becomes trapped by snowdrifts on the rails, in a blizzard, in the middle of nowhere. They realize cannibalism is the only way to survive, and dutifully follow parliamentary procedure to nominate and elect the next meal.

> *"After breakfast we elected a man by the name of Walker, from Detroit, for supper. He was very good. I wrote his wife so afterward. He was worthy of all praise. I shall always remember Walker. He was a little rare, but very good. And then the next morning we had Morgan of Alabama for breakfast. He was one of the finest men I ever sat down to, handsome, educated, refined, spoke several languages fluently. He was a perfect gentleman, and singularly juicy."*

Luckily, we were equipped with a well-stocked bar car to provide sustenance and entertainment when we tired of the featureless landscape. Most passengers waited patiently till about 4 o'clock, then began to congregate for socialization, food, and drink. Les and I were fortunate to be adopted by a retired French-Canadian railroad man. We were fascinated to find that he could ride the rails for free, anytime, and anywhere, as a retirement benefit. That sounded much more appealing than a life as a doctor, especially after four exhausting years of medical school.

He was a classic old timer – buy him a Molson, and he'd tell you his story. He was a thin, scruffy but kind-faced man, with alert eyes. I had experienced the same kind of pensioner in Missoula, Montana, where the bars are adorned with photos of the old-timers who built the infrastructure of the area, in this case the copper mines of Butte. You could hear fascinating stories and tall tales not described in dull history books, all for the price of a carefully nursed beer, often told by those pictured on the walls. This railroad

pensioner told his stories with a practiced decorum; he was
not boring, nor did he show his liquor as he carefully sipped
his beer. In medical school, we were trained to listen carefully to people's histories, and after an evening of stories, I
retired to my seat to sleep, and to dream railroad dreams.

The next morning, I was awakened from a deep sleep by
someone poking my arm. After momentary disorientation,
I remembered where I was, as I looked out at Canada passing by the window, accompanied by the sound of moving
rail wheels on track. I turned in the direction of the poke
to see the pensioner, smiling and nudging me with a hot
coffee in a Styrofoam cup. He was getting off at the next stop
and was thanking me for the beer and conversation and to
wish me well on my journey. After he left, I settled back in
my seat, propelled through time and space, watching myself
watching the western plains of Canada move past me.

The North American plains entice me. I've never been a
big city boy—I was born and raised in the oxbow of a river
in Fort Worth, a town whose motto is, "Where the West
Begins," in this case, the beginning of the desolate plains
of West Texas. Cities are interesting to visit, but the plains,
with blowing tumbleweeds, where not much can live, have
always been deeply satisfying to me. Time slows down there,
just like the pace of life on the train.

I was nevertheless looking forward to seeing the Canadian Rockies. Unfortunately, it was dark in Jasper when we
arrived. Passengers could leave the train for a half hour or so
while people got on and off. I had hoped to see what could
be seen of the Rockies at night, but it was just like any other
train station in the dark. As we de-trained, Reechard, a
French-Canadian we had met in the bar car, approached us.

"Eh, you want to get stoned?"

I loved the way he spoke Canadian with a French accent, and loved that he was Reechard, and not Richard. "But of course!" we laughed, taking on his local French-Canadian dialect. So stoned we got, in the dark of night at a train station in the Canadian Rockies. And, as it turned out, for a few stops after that. It seemed to be a very matter of fact occurrence, perhaps that is what everyone did at train stops in Canada. It was fun hearing of life as a French Canadian, and at the end of our last smoke before Vancouver, Reechard leaned close to us and said, "When you guys get to Vancouver, you have to go to the Gastown Inn."

By the time we got to Vancouver, I had almost forgotten why we had come. Les and I had spent seventy-one hours on the train without changing clothes or washing. We walked directly from the train station to Vancouver General Hospital, where we showed up dirty, smelly, and wearing our backpacks, as if we had just hitch-hiked cross-country to get there. Undaunted and confident, we planned to use our McGill experience to set the tone.

We approached a strikingly similar administrative assistant, who I am sure smelled us before she looked up to see two hippie-like, dirty-haired vagabonds. We declared confidently that we were American medical students, who had come to apply to their program, and work for them.

She took a brief look at us, the hint of a frown on her otherwise friendly countenance, and politely responded,

"We're not taking American medical students."

Her look conveyed that there would be no further negotiation.

"Could we talk with the person who makes appointments for interviews?"

"That would be me."

We were ready with our next line, "OK, how about we stay at the interns' quarters tonight so we can get cleaned up, and we'll be out of your hair tomorrow."

"We're not taking American medical students."

"Right, but can you direct us to the intern's quarters so we can get cleaned up."

"No."

This wasn't going as planned. We were with a skilled negotiator who was not going to budge from her position. We looked at each other, thanked her, and turned around and left. Now what were we going to do? Pay for a hotel room? No way!

"Let's try something," I said to Les. On the way out of the lobby, there was an information booth. We walked up and announced, "We're American medical students interviewing for an internship tomorrow, and they told us in administration we could stay overnight in the interns' quarters. Where would that be?"

We were politely directed to the house staff quarters, where there was an office that managed lodging. We repeated our lie: "We're American medical students applying for internship, and administration sent us over to get a room for the night, so we can interview tomorrow."

"Sure," the friendly Canadian said. Pleased with our Yankee ingenuity, we headed to our room, took a shower, changed clothes, and set out to locate the Gastown Inn.

The Gastown Inn was a large, airy bar and grill with open seating. It seemed like a normal lunch spot, with a standard menu. As we drank a beer and waited for food, we were a bit perplexed at Reechard's mandate, until we were interrupted by a man walking up to our table with a cigar box held at waist level by a strap that went around his neck. He opened the box to reveal his merchandise – joints, ounces of marijuana, and hashish. We weren't buyers that night, mainly because we would be crossing the border the next day, but Canada was turning out to be much more interesting than, say, Georgia, where you could be pulled over by the State Police for the crime of having long hair, and perhaps have it cut for you. Canada was a different world entirely.

So far we had stopped at two programs without making it past the front desk. Seattle was more of the same for me, as it turned out UW did not have the Family Practice program I was looking for. That left nothing for me to do, although Les did apply to UW's internal medicine program. All I remember of Seattle was visiting Les's brother Ralph's law office. His practice was so new, and he was so broke, that he couldn't afford furniture. Desk papers lay on the floor, occupying the space a desktop would take, and Les and I sat on the floor around his "desk," as there were no chairs. I wondered how impressive that must have been for his clients, but it turned out his clients at the time were legal aid, and didn't care if he had a desk.

*　*　*

WE WERE RUNNING OUT OF TIME AND MONEY, AND MY original plan to visit four schools was now down to one: Portland's Oregon Health Sciences University. We had vastly underestimated the distance between Portland and San Francisco and had no time to travel there and get back to Vancouver for the railway trip home. I had yet to participate in a single interview. However, I was finally in Oregon, and confident that this would be my new home. After all, I actually had a scheduled interview! I began ramping up to make a great impression, at what looked like my one and only choice. Better make it good.

We arrived in Portland midday, with my interview scheduled for the next day. The school had arranged for us to stay in the interns' quarters, so we did not need our practiced song and dance. That evening, after a night on the town, we were ushered to the interns' quarters by the Family Practice resident assigned to us. It didn't take him long before he started cursing the program, saying that it was horrible, demeaning, and that I shouldn't apply there. Uh-oh. He was convincing, but maybe he was just a sleep-deprived resident. Perhaps the interview would change my mind. However, it was a worrisome first impression.

My interview was with Dr. Miller, the head of the University's infectious disease program. He was white-coated and arrogant, and it appeared that interviewing potential new house staff was beneath his level of self-importance. His style was to make me uncomfortable, and demonstrate how much I didn't know, and how much he did. I was to find out years later that he had the reputation of being that way to just about everyone something that was unfortunately a bit too common in medical education. But Dr. Miller was the straw I had drawn.

He began asking me questions, all meant to test my knowledge base, as opposed to my character, or likelihood of success in their program. As the interview continued, I was really thinking about what I was going to do next, since this was the end of the road. I had been warned off the program by someone who should know, and now was being exposed to someone I disliked intensely.

I felt I was holding my own in the interview, yet I couldn't wait to have it over with, so I could contemplate

     As Fate Would Have It

what my next steps might be. I became less and less engaged in trying to make a good impression. Sensing my disinterest, Dr. Miller asked one last question that I had not anticipated: "Why do salmon die?"

Rather than take a guess, then be required to defend my thinking, I simply responded, "I don't know."

Having failed to engage me in a conversation in which he could rip apart my thinking, he continued, "Well, then, how would you design an experiment to determine why salmon die?"

If I had done my homework, I would have found that Dr. Miller was in fact the person who had discovered why salmon die. Then, I might have anticipated the question, and provide an impressive and brilliant answer. But by this time, I knew this place was not for me, and I was done playing his game. I smiled. "I don't know, but I sure would do a lot of fishin'!"

He stared unsmilingly at me and dismissively responded, "Thank you, Dr. Jefferson." The interview was over. I rose to leave the room without thanking him for this immense opportunity of having an audience with His Highness, but he persisted, apparently annoyed that I wasn't taking him seriously. "Don't you want to know why salmon die?"

I really didn't, and believe I just looked at him blankly. After all, of what possible use could it be to know that?

But he had to tell me. It was his claim to fame. This part of the interview was about him, not me.

"Adrenal exhaustion."

"That's interesting," I lied. Although once I thought about it, it was obvious. Salmon are incredible beings, with their instinctive and ultimately deadly urge to fight ocean cur-rents, then strong river currents, to head to quieter spawning grounds, then die. If you've ever had one on a line, you can sense their power and determination. Of course they die of exhaustion. They use themselves up, in one of those dramatic cycles of nature.

In retrospect, I wished I had said something wittier. I could visualize myself in an alternative universe, matter-of-factly answering his question "Why do salmon die?" with the accurate answer, "They die of exhaustion." "That's right, son! Brilliant! Welcome to OHSU!" As if it weren't obvious that we all ultimately die of exhaustion, having exhausted our resources to keep on living.

That was in the alternative universe. In the real universe, end of interview, and end of my plan to go to OHSU. I didn't even apply. Goodnight, Irene.

*　*　*

Les also had an interview that morning and was similarly uninterested in OHSU's internal medicine program, having his eyes mostly set on Seattle. We returned to our room and discussed strategy. We had travelled over 3000 miles, talked to four programs, and I wasn't applying to any of them. We were out of time and money. What next?

We opened the residency manual to investigate other programs and found a program across town at Emanuel Hospital that we had missed, so sure had we been that OHSU would be the answer. We called and scheduled an interview for the next day. It turned out to be just the right program for me – a rotating internship that would allow moving to a specific specialty program after one year, putting off a residency decision for another year. Gratifyingly, Emanuel appeared to be similarly interested in me. I left Oregon with some hope that I might return someday.

The plan I hatched on the front porch, reading *Sometimes A Great Notion,* came to fruition. I chose Emanuel, and Emanuel chose me, and I wouldn't have had it any other way. And I am still in Oregon forty-five years later, enjoying the particular set of circumstances that led me here.

The Lone Ranger

The first time I went fishing in Oregon, I ended up being held up at gunpoint.

The summer of 1973 I moved to Portland, Oregon to begin my internship at Emanuel Hospital. I took every chance to take a break from the brutal working schedule to explore my new surroundings. I had never lived in a place that featured snow-capped mountains and such beautiful rivers. At the time I fancied myself a fly fisherman, and days off were spent exploring the spots where the great fish lived. The thought of hooking a steelhead with fly gear led me to a much-anticipated weekend on the Deschutes River. And so it was off to the arid, remote, and rugged desert town of Maupin, population 400, to camp, fish, and reflect alongside the great river draining the eastern portion of the Cascade Mountains, as it carried its massive snowmelt into the Columbia River.

The last stretch of the trip was a pothole-filled gravel road that paralleled the swiftly moving Deschutes River. As I gazed from the rolled-down window of my VW Bug at the watery spectacle, and wondered how fish could survive or be hooked in such a current, my car suddenly ground to a halt. Oddly, my left front tire continued bouncing down the gravel road as if there were still a car attached to it, seemingly drawn to a watery fate. The tire bounded down a slight embankment and into the river, never to be seen again.

The tire was gone, my hopes of fishing dashed, the front rim of my VW demolished. The tow truck driver from nearby Madras informed me, after quick inspection, that I had two choices: I could stay in Madras for a couple of days until a new front rim could be delivered from Portland, or he could hammer and hacksaw the crimps from my front rim, put on another tire, and I could drive back to Portland for further repair. The latter choice came with a wrinkle: with an incomplete rim and without the VW's front-wheel brakes, I would only have a hand brake operational for the 120-mile drive back to Portland.

I had to be back to work on Monday, so after some delay to chop up my car, I returned to Portland using only the car's handbrake. It was an anxious trip home, but easier than anticipated. I reflected that the weekend had been more about adventure than catching fish, and it had not been dull. The escapade was over, and I had a new and unusual fishing tale of the ones that got away.

Back in Portland on Monday and needing to have my Bug's front rim and brake repaired, I borrowed a friend's bicycle, strapped it to the top of the car, and drove to an auto repair shop about ten blocks away, hoping to make a quick drop-off during our lunch break. Our hospital, and the auto repair shop, was in a dangerous area of North Portland, but I was oblivious to that at the time.

As I was leaving the garage and began to mount the bicycle to ride back to work, I found it difficult getting into the toe clips of the unfamiliar bike and leaned up against a parked mail truck to adjust them.

As I was adjusting the clips, I felt a presence near me, then heard a soft but gruffly determined voice, "Get off that bike."

The speaker was a young black man, about my size. To show he meant business, he flashed a pistol from his jacket pocket. I stared blankly, trying to take in the situation. He repeated, "Give me your bike."

Over the years I have often wondered what then possessed me, and why I responded as I did.

"Actually, it's my friend's bike. It's not my bike to give you."

He looked perplexed by a response that was grounded in reason rather than fear. "Give me your bike," he repeated with increasing intensity, as if I had not understood his initial demand.

From a strange place within me, I replied, "What do you want with it?"

He was momentarily distracted and began to engage in the developing conversation. "I need to get to a friend's house."

I suppose in the spirit of neighborliness, I heard myself say, "Well, hop on, I'll give you a ride."

That apparently was not an acceptable compromise; living in brotherhood was not his goal for the day. Realizing the conversation wasn't going the way he wanted, and apparently frustrated by my failure to grasp that I was being held up at gunpoint, he moved forward quickly and slugged me in the jaw, knocking me to the ground. The bike, which I was still gripping by the handlebars, fell with me. I picked myself and the bike up.

At that point my entire perspective narrowed to the field of vision enclosing my assailant, myself, and the bike. At this crucial moment, the driver of the mail truck against which I had been leaning, appeared in the periphery, now triangulating the confrontation. Out of the corner of my eye, I sensed that he looked at me and said, "Do you need any help?"

Without taking my eyes off the man with the gun, I responded, "No, this is between him and me." It was as if, disembodied, I was watching the drama unfold. The mailman, probably relieved that I had given him permission to avoid helping out, withdrew from the scene.

With this clarification of the participants in the standoff, I suggested a potential solution that might work for both of us. "I'll tell you what. I can't give you the bike, but I can give you twenty bucks." I knew I had a Jackson in my wallet.

He briefly considered this, then nodded in agreement. I pulled out my wallet. As I opened it, to my horror and his delight, I saw I had two twenties instead of one. He snatched the wallet from my hand, and I instinctively I grabbed it back, not wanting to lose my entire wallet when all I had offered was a twenty. I thought we had reached an agreement.

That put him over the edge. "I'm really going to have to shoot you," he said. He started backing away from me, looking up and down the street to see who might witness a shooting, as he reached into his pocket for the gun.

When I saw him looking around, I knew exactly what my next move would be. It wasn't more conversation.

In the fifties, the TV set had been my babysitter, and I watched more than a fair amount of TV. Growing up in Texas, and wanting to be a cowboy, I was particularly attracted to Westerns. And in that category, there was one figure that stood out above them all: The Lone Ranger.

The Lone Ranger was a Texas Ranger, the ultimate cowboy in my nascent Texan mind. In my naïve childhood there were no men more heroic than the Texas Rangers. They were the personification of the struggle between good and evil, and the Lone Ranger was the best of them all. He was akin to Zorro, Robin Hood, and Superman, the other favorites of my childhood. Each had their distinctive skillsets, or superpowers, in their job to assure justice in a world filled with malcontents.

The masked man didn't drink, smoke, or hang out in bars. He spoke cultured English, never shot to kill, and defended those who could not defend themselves. The world of romance, love, and loss were foreign to him, as his mission was truth and justice, to the accompaniment of Rossini's William Tell Overture and the stirring voice-over…

> *"A fiery horse with the speed of light, a cloud of dust and a hearty Hi-Yo Silver! The Lone Ranger!…With his faithful Indian companion Tonto, the daring and resourceful masked rider of the plains led the fight for law and order in the early western United States! Nowhere in the pages of history can one find a greater champion of justice! Return with us now to those thrilling days of yesteryear! From out of the past come the thundering hoofbeats of the great horse Silver! The Lone Ranger rides again!"*

I learned many tricks from the Lone Ranger, who was in plenty of fist fights. And somehow, there on that Portland street, I realized that the young gunman and I were playing out a Lone Ranger episode. It hadn't been me talking, I had been channeling the Lone Ranger. Waiting for my chance.

The Lone Ranger had a consistent move whenever the bad guy was getting ready to brandish his weapon or trying to get the drop on him. Grab the gun hand and beat the hand against a rock until the gun fell to the ground. This reduced the standoff to a fistfight, which the Lone Ranger always won.

As my bad guy began looking around for witnesses to the upcoming shooting, he made a crucial mistake, instinctively noticed by my modern-day Ranger. He took his eyes off me, allowing me, at long last, to get the jump on him. The advantage had shifted. I made my move. In a flash I literally visualized and played out the details of the television wash where I had learned this trick. I rushed him, grabbed the hand with the gun, and because there were no rocks around, planned to beat his gun hand against a nearby parked car.

Things turned out differently than the TV episode. He immediately wrested his hand from my clutch and chose, rather than to shoot me, to hit me on the head with the butt of the gun.

Apparently one of my superpowers is being hard-headed. It came in handy that day. When he struck me on the head, he lost control of the gun, and it clattered to the ground. When I heard, then saw, the gun on the ground, I grabbed the guy in an adrenalin-powered bear hug, locked my arms around him in a death grip, and didn't let go. I could have held on to him for a long time, I believe. But I didn't need to.

Two men jumped out of nowhere and pulled me off him. One of them, apparently a friend of my accoster, picked up the gun and pocketed it. I looked around and there I was, bleeding from the previous blow to the cheek, bicycle on the ground, now with maybe fifteen people standing around us in a circle, all yelling. From the rising din I could hear one older woman shouting, "We don't want no guns on our streets!"

I had no idea where the crowd came from. I can only assume the mailman stuck around, and a crowd had gathered to see how the fight would come out, not knowing until this last moment that he had a gun.

I took a look at the crowd, one look at the young man and his two friends and jumped on the bike. I took off straight over a curb and began pedaling as fast as I could. Hi Yo Silver! I blew the back tire out going over the curb but kept pedaling the mile or so back to work on the flat tire, without stopping, and now, for the first time, terrified.

Later that night, a woman and her husband were held up at gunpoint by a man of the same description, in the same part of town. He shot her in the abdomen, but she survived. I hoped it wasn't the frustrated young man, but I feared that it was.

I often wonder who I really am, when all the parental scripting, media influences, and life experiences are stripped away. As if that is even possible. In this instance, because the man was about my size, I suppose I thought I could hold my own with him in a fair fight. But that didn't occur to me at the time. My words and actions weren't intentionally strategic; they came from a deep sense of survival, of knowing what to do. Of course, others who have doubtless thought their instincts could save their lives, ended up dying with that last thought. I do not discount the luck factor, the playing out of fate. My fate that day was mystically linked with the fictitious and always victorious Lone Ranger.

Perhaps it was because of my early years in the spotlight, singing love songs while frightened by the monster with the red eye, that hardened me to terrifying situations. Some inner me took over with calm intellectualization, plotting my escape in the battle between good and evil, life and death, where love and loss were temporarily on vacation. I instinctively sang love to my opponent, and when that failed, another persona, the Lone Ranger, magically appeared to bail me out.

I was the masked man, hiding a truer, previously unrevealed identity. One who knew he could negotiate the struggle between good and evil.

The fishing trip was now concluded. I had sought adventure in hunting creatures, and found myself the one being hunted. The fish and river gods, then the Lone Ranger, conspired to let me off the hook, to live another day.

But who was that masked man?

The River Virgin

Having grown up in the flatlands of Fort Worth, where mineral-tinged, tepid brown water ran faster from a faucet than down a river, I found the rivers of Oregon to be incredibly beautiful, and as cold as the snowmelt they originated from. And so, when I was invited on my first trip down an Oregon river, I was both excited and wary.

As an intern at Emanuel Hospital in Portland, I found myself hanging out with the orderlies and ward clerks rather than with my fellow interns. After all, the hospital employees were locals; the interns came from all over the country. Coming from Texas via Virginia, I found the agreeableness of the West Coast to be in stark contrast to the parochialism I had recently left in the Good Ol' Boys South. I wanted to experience my new home with local, down-to-earth people. And I was interested in learning and living the lifestyle of Oregonians, now that I was one.

And so it was that I fell in with Forest, who had been born and raised in Portland. As an orderly, Forest was starting at one of the lowest rungs of hospital employment. Orderlies had low paying, physically demanding jobs. Patient cleanup was one of their roles, which was often unpleasant. But it was a job with benefits, and it was never boring. One of the fascinations of life in a hospital is that no day is like the previous, amazing events occur, and stories abound. Hospital workers are known to have a dark sense of humor, as there are plenty of horrific stories, among the many uplifting ones. You get to see people at their worst, and at their most grateful. You learn the benefits of teamwork, and how to manage the arrogant, the frightened, and the dying.

My sense of humor matched Forest's, and we became friends. In March, it was Forest that asked me if I wanted to go tubing with him and his brothers down the Estacada River. Sure, I said nervously. Picking up on the hesitation, he smiled as he found out I had never floated an Oregon river, and informed me that I would thus be referred to as a river virgin, and of course something needed to be done about that. I was reminded of this fact often enough during the buildup to the actual trip that, by the time of the trip itself, I was excitedly anticipating the loss of my virginity.

I knew nothing of the insanity of tubing down an Oregon river in March. First of all, I had to clarify what he meant by tubing, and yes, it was to go down the river in truck sized inner tubes, which would be supplied by Forest and his brothers. No boats; no rafts. He warned me that the water would be very cold, requiring wetsuits, so off I went to a scuba store. As I tried on the suit, I felt claustrophobic. Tight spaces and tight clothing gave me the willies, but it was required dress for my date with destiny.

⋆　⋆　⋆

THE DAY FINALLY ARRIVED TO MEET AT THE PUT-IN AND start the trip, which I understood would consist of floating several miles downriver before we took out. There were four of us, each with our own inner tube. I had no idea what to do, but the routine was simple. They had already arranged the pickup vehicle, so our job at the embarkation beach was to don wetsuits, kid each other, and generally do man stuff, which meant assuming a confident and jocular façade to cover one's anxieties. Forest's brothers brought a separate inner tube for beer. I was surprised, and a bit apprehensive, that the last ritual before hitting the river was to pass around a flask of whiskey and toast the coming loss of my virginity, even though it was mid-morning. His brothers were quite garrulous, crazier and more reckless than Forest, but I got the feeling they knew what they were doing. After all, they were blue collar linebacker type guys with trucks. Boisterousness was their way of life. What could possibly go wrong?

They told me the river was higher than usual, since we'd had a particularly wet winter, and the snowpack was deep. As we pushed off our inner tubes from the small beach, I was overcome with the enormity and power of the water, smooth and slow on the surface, but with a major current beneath. Off we went on that sunny, chilly day. With our hands, we paddled out to a smooth patch in the middle of the river, where they showed me how to maneuver and use my feet to push away from rocks.

My anxiety faded as we began the float. It was wonderful to lie in the inner tube and feel the sun bake me in my wetsuit. We stayed together for a while, passing beers and joints around. Life was good. This is what Oregon and Oregon rivers were about: pleasant drifting with friends.

After a while, the pace quickened. I noticed that I was floating away from the others, me going on one side of a large island, they on the other. I shouted at them as to what to do; they said no worries; the river would come back together downstream. And so I continued my luxuriating drift, now on my own to contemplate my good fortune, to feel the sun, to relax, and reflect on my new life in Oregon. Did it get any better than this?

* * *

AFTER A WHILE, I NOTICED THE RIVER PICKING UP EVEN more steam, and wondered what was to come next. An unfamiliar roar was now audible. I wondered what the source of the sound was, but now being on my own, there was no one to ask.

The quickening current turned to whitewater, and it seemed I was now going downhill. It was all I could do to keep myself straight, to not twirl around. As the island ended, my fork of the river took a major left turn. I was now in serious rapids, heading straight toward a carved out earthy bank of the river as the two channels merged at a ninety-degree angle. Things were happening fast, and the sound of rushing water was all that could be heard. I was being ferried straight into the bank. Putting my legs out to take on the impact, I forcefully hit the tree-root-entangled dirt wall with my feet and successfully pushed off, only to find myself in a large pool, slowly drifting towards a waterfall.

This was not good. Crazily, I began back paddling away from the waterfall, as if I could back-paddle up the river in my inner tube, just using my arms. There was no way out; I was going over the falls.

Going over the waterfall, I had no idea how far the drop would be, whether there were rocks beneath, or what I should do. Things happened so quickly that there was no time for planning, so I reacted instinctively. After all, I had not been briefed on proper technique for going over a waterfall in an inner tube.

As I reached the top of the waterfall, I could see the narrowed river dropped about eight feet into a hole. As I went over, then hit the bottom of the hole, I was tossed from the inner tube and went underwater. Luckily, I had the presence of mind to hook my arm around one side of the tube, and its ballast kept me from going further under, and from who-knows-what fate if I had not. They had not mentioned this safety precaution, but things were happening so rapidly, it was sheer instinct to hold onto something that could keep me near the surface.

My dunking at the base of the waterfall happened so quickly, that the next thing I knew, I was floating down the river again, this time in the river, with one arm wrapped around the tube. Forest and his brothers had preceded me over the falls and were all watching to see what would happen to me. The river beyond the waterfall was placid again, allowing me to climb back into the safety of the rubber torus. Then we drifted to a place to beach and regroup.

Although they had been down this section of river before, they had never gone down it in such high water, so the waterfall was a surprise to them also. We all sat shivering on the beach for a while as we exchanged with each other what our experience had been like, and what was going through our minds.

Forest's fear as he went over the waterfall was that the water could take him into some sort of intake pipe, where he would get wedged and die. Glad I didn't think of that. I hadn't done any thinking at all, just responded to the situation, which seemed to have worked.

We sat on the beach for a while, trading stories and downing shots from the flask of whiskey, which had miraculously made it through the waterfall, and waiting for the adrenalin to dissipate so we could continue the journey, which turned out from that point to be uneventful.

As the fear waned and our heart rates returned to normal, we reached a point where there was no more to tell, and silence emerged as we all turned inward. There followed a period of resting quietly and reflecting, each of us splayed out in our inner tubes on the beach, each in our respective ways thanking our lucky stars, with no sound but the river and the trees. Sometime into the reverie, Forest broke the silence. He casually looked over at me, and drawled dryly, "Well, TJ, you're no longer a river virgin. You just got fucked!"

We all got a good laugh at that. True enough, I thought. But that was the last time I went looking for excitement with that particular crew.

Forest and I remained friends, though after I left Emanuel I didn't hear from him for a few years. Then one day, after I had started my career in family medicine, he called to let me know he had worked his way up from orderly and was now in Physician Assistant's school. Would I agree to sponsor him in an externship in my office for three months as part of his training? I jumped at the chance to help him along with his career. It was great to see him again, and great to re-live, with our staff, the story of my loss of virginity.

Water, Water, Everywhere

————∞————

I am a Leo, a fire sign. Some say water douses fire. It continued to try.

My first memory of water was being flung through the air, arcing backwards into the Fort Worth municipal pool. My father, a champion at diving into water from the low board without a splash, apparently felt that my best introduction to water was to toss me in. Sink or swim. As I was airborne, watching the smile on his face, I remember thinking in horror, "What?" My plagued relationship with water had begun.

A few years later, as adults grouped and chatted and children played on the sidewalk outside of church, I overheard a tragic story. One of the women in the church, with her daughter in the front seat, had driven her car off the road into a river. This was in the early days of seat belts, and the daughter got free, but the mother could not. Her daughter repeatedly went to the surface for air and dived back into the water to detach her mother's seat belt, to no avail, and her mother drowned. I have no idea why parents would let their children hear stories like that. The image of the woman drowning while clutching at her seat belt still lingers. When I first started driving many years later, I would not wear a seat belt, haunted by that image. The thought of drowning terrified me, although I didn't really dwell on death itself, just the drowning part. It wasn't death, it was the dying that got my attention.

* * *

IN MY TWENTIES, WHILE VISITING FRIENDS IN BERKELEY on a hot summer day, we went to one of the public lakes in the nearby hills. On the shore, I imagined the great accomplishment of swimming across the lake. There was a floating wooden dock about a quarter of the way across, and my hastily devised plan was to swim out to the dock, rest, then dive in, glide through the water for as long as I could, then swim to the other side.

I made it to the dock without incident, an easy swim. After resting briefly, I gathered my courage to jump into the unknown, and in my anxiety, my plan immediately went awry. I had neglected to consider my attire, and as I dived from the dock, my loosely fitting cutoff jean shorts slipped down to my ankles, exposing my underwear-less body. I struggled to pull them up, while watching to see if anyone at the dock was noting my embarrassing condition. Flustered, yet undaunted in my goal, but now with precious energy expended, I set out for the distant shore from a dog paddle start just a few feet from the dock.

The next flaw in my plan, was that I didn't know how to swim. Somehow, that had not occurred to me as being a problem. I was young, athletic, and invincible. It wasn't the English Channel. How hard could it be? Very hard, it turned out. Halfway to the opposite shore, I began to tire. My muscles wouldn't work anymore, and I began to struggle just to keep my head above water. I was panicking and realized this could be what the initial stages of drowning must be like. I needed help.

I knew that the lake had a lifeguard but could not bring myself to call for help. I apparently thought it was better to drown than to be embarrassed about what a fool I was, although I can't say that crossed my mind at the time. I could see the rapidly upcoming juncture where I could struggle no more. I realized I was going to die right there in a city lake, with hundreds of people around, including a lifeguard, but that was the way it was going to be. It was between me and the water.

I decided then and there to give myself up to the universe, to offer my body and being to the unknown. I spread my arms out to greet whatever came next and, with open arms, thought, this is it, take me, it's over. It was one of the most spiritual moments of my life.

As I lay on my back, arms and legs outspread, opening myself to the universe…….I realized I was floating. I was being held by the water. I didn't have to struggle. When I realized I wasn't going to die, tears flowed down my cheeks and washed into the lapping wavelets. There I was, floating on my back in the middle of a lake, crying with thanks to the life-giving spirit of nature.

I did an occasional slow backstroke to eventually glide to shore. I realized the journey was over when my back scraped the bottom of the lake and I beached in the shallows. I rested for a moment on my back, rolled over, and crawled out of the lake, as I imagined the first fish that emerged from the ocean might have done. I sat on the beach for a while to regain my strength, then took a trail around the lake to my departure point, where my friends queried, "How was it?"

"It was quite an experience." That was all I could come up with. And it was the truth.

Since that time, I decided that when faced with death, I would give myself fully to the experience. To struggle was to die; to merge was to live. As it turned out, I had additional opportunities to practice this technique.

*   *   *

In my thirties, I set out with friends and strangers, to raft Oregon's Crooked River. It was a guided trip, and there were ominous signs from the beginning.

I was a family physician at the time, and the nature of my work acquainted me with many individuals with difficult lives. One family stood out. The father was a Vietnam vet with significant PTSD, trying hard to support his family. He had been wounded in battle, and in the ambulance on the way to the field hospital, from the stretcher above him, a severed head dropped and rolled onto the floor. He could understandably not get the horror of that experience from his mind. It constantly replayed, in waking and in dreams. His wife was exhausted and depressed, having to deal not only with her husband's stress, but with being the main breadwinner and caregiver for their two boys, ten and twelve years old at the time. One was very intelligent, the great hope of their family; the other boy had a severe developmental disability, requiring constant and special attention. They were a hard-working family, fervently trying to make the best of their lives. The father took what jobs he could, usually manual labor, but his physical and mental battle wounds kept him from keeping any job for too long.

On arriving at the meeting point for the raft trip, I was surprised to find that he was one of the guides. I knew for a fact he had little to no experience on the river, as we regularly discussed his work history. We were both surprised to see each other, and we both independently decided it was best to keep our relationship confidential, so few words were spoken between us. But I was uneasy that my life, and the lives of others, could be in his hands, though that thought was quickly forgotten as the trip began.

All went well the first day. The Crooked River flow at the time made for technical maneuvering but was not dangerous. We camped along the river that night, eagerly anticipating our second and final day of the trip, which we knew was more dangerous.

The next morning, as we got in our rafts, I looked up into the beautiful sunlit sky and noticed two contrails crossing, forming a gigantic "X" in the direction we were headed. The "X" took up the entire sky. I pointed it out and remember joking to others, saying, Well, that's a good sign. They laughed weakly and nervously, letting me know that might have been best kept to myself.

The most difficult part of the day was the final set of rapids. At the end of the rapids was the takeout; the trip would then be over. It was to be a thrilling finale. The end of our adventure was where the Crooked River Bridge, also known as Baby Bridge, crossed the river.

The bridge got its name in 1961, when two young children were flung some 350 feet from the bridge into the deep Crooked River gorge below by their mother. I heard this disturbing story for the first time as we paused to scout the path we would take from the head of the rapids towards the site of that calamity, the bridge an arching end of the trip. The signs of trouble were everywhere.

After some deliberation, and with building anxiety, we decided on our path through the rapids, climbed in the raft, and entered the treacherous water. We had gone no farther than fifty feet when we got stuck on an unseen underwater boulder. The rock was sticking up in the middle of the raft, holding us motionless. We were unmoving amidst a massive torrent. The temporary motionlessness provided us an opportunity to discuss the best way to proceed. We decided to inch ourselves off the rock by slowly moving some in the raft forward, moving our center of gravity. We moved slowly at first, then the front of the raft suddenly tipped forward under the shifted weight. The rushing water under the rear of the raft flipped us all upside down into the rapids.

We had been schooled in proper technique if you dumped in. Get your feet out in front of you to steer and push off rocks, face downriver, and hope for the best. What I had not been schooled in was what happened next.

As we dumped into the river, the woman next to me grabbed my arm in a death grip. She was panicked, screaming for help, and, despite my life vest, began holding me underwater to keep herself afloat, as the raft floated away from us and took its own path downstream.

I know now I should have taken charge of the situation, forcefully grabbing and holding her in front of me so that we could tandem down the rapids, feet in front. But I didn't know that then. And there wasn't much time to come up with a plan: we were careening downriver in rock-filled whitewater.

She and I washed past a rock into an eddy. We were now suddenly in a pool, no longer plunging down the rapids. She continued to hold me under water to keep herself above water. Oddly, I felt like I was helping her by not resisting. I remember looking up through the water at the sky, saying to myself, *I'm going to die here*. There were no other thoughts or actions. I didn't resist. Then the sounds and sights faded.

The next thing I knew, I was being pulled from the river into the other raft that had preceded us down the rapids. They hauled me aboard, then slogged me to shore where I coughed up a bunch of water, while the others took turns warming me up with their bodies. I was finally settled enough to get into the car, as that was the takeout site, and it was from there we would ride home, first crossing Baby Bridge. I stared down into the river, where others before me had drowned.

Once again, I had given myself up to a watery grave, only to emerge shaken, but whole. I have no idea how we got out of the eddy, and no one in our party did either. The woman left immediately with her friends. I tried to get in touch with her afterwards to discuss the experience, but she did not respond to my queries.

* * *

During those years, I had the good fortune to have a close relationship with a Tibetan lama and physician, Chagdud Tulku. He had taught me Phowa, the Tibetan method of ejecting one's consciousness at the time of death, and I believed I was prepared for the process of death. I was curious that this near-death experience had simply been a voice inside my head that was calmly saying, and knowing, that I was going to die. No struggle, just a giving in to the situation and an acceptance of death. There were no bright lights, no rising up and floating around, no gods or demons, no life flashing before my eyes, no activity whatsoever. Just, I am going to die here.

Thankfully, the voice was wrong. I was struck with the simplicity of what could have been my last thought. It made me wonder what others' last thoughts might be. There are many collections of people's last words, but of course not of last thoughts. That would be interesting, revealing, and helpful to know.

One result of these experiences, and of being formally trained in the experience of death, is that I don't fear death. I know what death will be like for me. It's old hat. Been there, done that. Just another death. Just like going to sleep and not waking up.

It is also possible that I was born without a fear of death, and these watery experiences just allowed that trait to manifest, to observe death as it nears. Either way, I am happy that I don't fear death. Many people do. For me, it's one less thing to worry about.

There has been another effect, no doubt an illusion. These near-death experiences have given me the strangest feeling that I did drown, but then washed up in an alternative universe in which my life continued. That this is all a dream. The mind, and life, is a strange and wonderful place.

The gods kept throwing me in the water, and I kept bobbing out.

The Dirty Shame Saloon

My love affair with Montana began the summer after my first year of med school. I was making a cross country trek from Virginia with a college buddy, who had just finished his Army tour. We had never visited the Great American West, and he had a friend in Missoula, so that was our destination.

The days in Missoula were magical. When we drove into town, his friend was still at work, so we settled into a local bar. It was a corner bar with open air entrances on two streets. As we sat having lunch and a cold beer, children and their dogs paraded through, cutting the corner. I immediately loved the West – the rules were different here. I felt free.

One day during our visit I headed out of town on my own to explore the Bitterroot Valley. I let my mind wander as I drove off in my '69 VW bug. I was so enthralled with the scenery that before I knew it, I had travelled a hundred miles, whereupon I saw a sign directing me through a forest to Big Hole National Battlefield.

A previous trip to Manassas Battlefield in Virginia had convinced me that battlefields were places that commanded reverence. An eerie wind seems to blow through battlefields, as if trying to sweep away the terror and carnage. But ghosts remain in the charnel ground, forever trapped in their liminal space, still trying to find their own and their loved one's bodies in a dream that doesn't end.

As the road through the Montana forest opened up in the valley of Big Hole, I paused on a rise to view the wide valley and big sky. I began to feel exactly like I did at Manassas, a sadness mixed with the absurdity of war. I had heard of Big Hole, but at the time did not know the circumstances. It did not matter, as the wind in its low-pitched exhalation through the valley spoke to me of the invisible suffering that had taken place there.

As I looked off into the distance, a long way up the valley, I could see a storm approaching. There were black clouds, lightning bolts striking the ground, rumbling thunder, and the translucent gray of rainfall stretching from cloud to ground. As the thunderstorm moved closer, I noticed that I could see all the way around the storm – it was a more or less circular, isolated weather cell surrounded by the sunlit beauty of the valley, a nexus of dark filled with lightning, moving slowly up the valley toward the battleground.

I felt like an eagle, flying over an auspicious place, witnessing the eons of history before humans arrived, then the first nomads, and then their destruction, with the wind, thunder, lightning and rain establishing their primacy. Montana had hooked me, and I knew I would return.

*　*　*

When I finished medical school, and then my internship, I had no idea what I wanted to do with my degree. My eyes had been opened to varied experiences: I had seen Piney River Smith trading medical services for hams in the Blue Ridge Mountains of Virginia; I had seen the poor black families appreciative of health care in central Virginia; I had seen the poverty and devastation of coal miners with black lung in Appalachian Tennessee. I wanted to go where I could be useful, which led me back to Montana, to the Indian Health Service.

The US government supported a medical clinic in Browning, Montana, on the Blackfoot reservation. I was anticipating being near the place where I had experienced that earlier transcendent day. But expectations were shattered as the Native American woman who interviewed me quickly cut to the chase. She listed the major problems: poverty, alcoholism, diabetes, and depression. She herself seemed depressed, and not all that interested in offering me employment. Perhaps she was just being honest, so as not to encourage this idealistic young doctor. I really don't remember much about the visit after that, as I knew right away this was not the environment for me. It was sad, but I really did not see how I could be anything but a cog in a beauracracy that wasn't making much of a difference, and that was funded by the government whose policies created the environment in which depression and alcoholism emerged. One hundred years of reservation detention had not improved the bitterness and suspicion. I knew I would always be an outsider who felt ashamed of his predecessors. This visit made clear to me that while I could love Montana, I was not a native. The magical spell of my first visit had been broken, revealing the bare bones of sorrow that lay beneath the beauty of Montana.

* * *

Years later, the Blackfoot reservation experience a distant memory, I was offered a third opportunity to visit Montana and further define our relationship. I was invited to make a weeklong bicycle trek with a dozen friends, travelling the Going to the Sun Road through Glacier National Park, then to Waterton Park in Canada, returning by way of Yaak, Montana. Partly due to my last visit, I was hesitant, until Tom, the trip leader, in the course of explaining the trip, mentioned that Yaak was the location of the Dirty Shame Saloon.

That did it for me: I couldn't quite picture myself cycling through Glacier Park, but I could picture myself in the Dirty Shame Saloon, even though I had never heard of it. My Tibetan friend Chagdud had recently been extoling the virtues of Tibetan yaks, the pleasures of yak butter tea, and the religious uses of yak butter lamps in shrines in the wilds of eastern Tibet. The association of The Dirty Shame Saloon and Yaak assured me in an illogical way that this was a trip I would not miss. I immediately began visualizing the day I would set foot in the Dirty Shame. Something transformative was going to happen there; getting there and returning were just details.

Jane and I, with our friends Ed and Jean, drove with our bikes and gear from Eugene to Whitefish, Montana, where we rendezvoused with the rest of the riders. We were a self-supporting trip, and had rented a U-Haul truck to take our camping gear from one campsite to the next, taking turns driving. Our camp reservations had been made in advance. All we needed on our bikes were snacks and various layering clothes for comfort. It was perfect for me, as hauling my own and my bike's weight up hills was the least favorite part of cycling for me. We weren't exactly in a flat part of the country.

We saddled up about mid-afternoon, and followed Tom, who knew the way. The first leg of the trip was along a highway, with cars and trucks whizzing by. There was a light rain, and the road was under construction, providing plenty of mud in the road spray. Given the rain, poor visibility, traffic, and grime, it was an extremely unpleasant twenty-five-mile beginning to my third visit to Montana. Fortunately, this was just the preliminary to get to the real start of the trip, in West Glacier, Montana, where the western end of the Going to the Sun Road winds upwards through beautiful Glacier Park for the next fifty miles. That day our spirits were uplifted by the sunny, majestic scenery. On this and subsequent days, we broke into several groups, mostly to match riders of the same ability, as we covered the mountainous terrain. We made a slow and pleasant meander to our campground at St. Mary, where the Going to the Sun Road ends. I had forgotten what motivated me to come on the trip in the first place and was pleased I had come. Once again natural beauty brought peace of mind.

The next day we would cover another fifty miles, going across the border to Waterton Park in Canada. Again we broke into groups, and I wandered at a leisurely pace with Jean and Sharon. They wanted to ride slowly and take it all in, and I was happy to ride with them. Our leisurely pace was broken by a very long, straight, steep downhill that led us to the Canadian border. It is the kind of downhill that can be thrilling, and dangerous. Although I hated biking uphill, I rationalized it was worth it, as my very favorite thing to do was speed downhill, and I was always trying to break my downhill speed record. We stopped at the top, screwed up our courage, and took off It was like gaining speed on the downhill of a ski jump, but hoping you don't end up flying through the air. On that downhill, I reached fifty-two mph –not a record, but scarily exhilarating. I learned later that

Sharon had stopped midway in tears, as it reminded her of the tragic death of a cyclist who, on a snowy downhill in the Oregon Cascades, went off the road and died when he hit a tree. Although this Montana terrain and conditions were nothing like wintertime Oregon, downhills were forever scary to her. It was a fun day for me, but not for Sharon.

Canadian national parks, unlike American national parks, have no entry fees, no reservations; you just show up and camp. We arrived and spread out in a beautiful flat and open area next to a large mountain lake. We all sat around a campfire, told our day's stories, and laughed till we all fell asleep.

* * *

THE NEXT MORNING MY EXCITEMENT BEGAN TO BUILD: this day would be a 100-mile ride, our longest of the trip, with the Dirty Shame Saloon at about the fifty-mile mark. We would get there around noon, perfect to ride into town and wash down the road dust with a visit to the town watering hole.

We had again split into a few groups, but stayed pretty close to each other. I was in the last group to arrive in Yaak, which turned out to be a convenience market on one corner, and the Dirty Shame Saloon on the other. As I rode up, I saw our group lounging on the grass outside the market, taking their lunch from what they had brought, or obtained in the store. To my surprise, I was the only one interested in visiting the Dirty Shame. Their loss, I thought. What did they come on this trip for?

I dismounted, tied my bike to the hitching post, adjusted from riding to walking legs, then clomped up the steps to the swinging doors of the saloon.

My favorite part of Westerns, whether novels or movies, are the barroom scenes in small towns. The main character, dusty and thirsty from a long ride, dismounts his horse at the local saloon and assertively announces himself with his bootsteps loud on the wooden steps. He walks through the swinging doors, pauses for a moment to get the layout of the room, then strides to the bar. He is the loner, the stranger in town. Sparse and simple dialog follows as the bartender and the bar patrons wonder just why the stranger is in town. What is his story?

This was precisely what I had visualized when I had heard of the Dirty Shame Saloon months earlier. This was why I was here. I could finally inhabit my dream role. I knew exactly what to do.

I wasn't exactly Clint Eastwood coming through the swinging doors in my dusty trail gear. I was shod not with boots, but narrow, form-fitting, clip-in bike shoes, whose cleats did however make the requisite sound on the wooden steps and floor of the saloon. My wardrobe did not include chaps, or a scruffy, dirty, sweat-stained wide-brimmed hat, or a neckerchief, or a trail coat – no, I entered in Spandex bike shorts and a brightly colored royal-blue tight-fitting nylon three-pocket road biking jersey.

So there I was, hot and thirsty, parting the doors and stopping to survey the scene. It was a classic Western bar, with a bartender and a couple of cowboys on barstools on each side of the bar. In the exact middle of the bar, a lone empty seat beckoned. The bar noise settled into a perfect quiet as the bartender looked up and the four cowboys swiveled their heads as one to see who it was. If there had been a piano player, he would have stopped playing to watch.

     As Fate Would Have It

I clomped up to the bar as the five men silently watched me take my seat. No words were spoken until I looked up at the bartender and spoke the line I had long anticipated.

"Whiskey."

The bartender looked at me, then slowly looked up at the whiskey selection behind the bar, wordlessly pointing with his eyes. I scanned the bottles and knew immediately what it would be.

"BlackJack."

He poured a shot of Jack Daniels Black Label and set it before me with the satisfying clunk of glass on the wooden bar. The cowboys and bartender watched and waited, anticipating how the scene might play out. As in my dream, I had the only lines so far.

The bartender stood with the bottle still in his hands as I tossed the shot down in one gulp, and clunked the glass down on the bar forcefully to reinforce that I wasn't done.

"Another one."

The bartender wordlessly poured another. This one was to enjoy, and as I began to take a sip from the shot glass, the cowboy on the barstool to my right broke the silence.

"Now that's what I like, a biker that drinks whiskey."

With the silence now broken, the plot took on a life of its own. My internal screenplay ended at the second whiskey; I had not thought through the rest of the scene. We settled into guy talk as I nursed the second shot, already feeling its effects after having just ridden fifty miles and not having eaten anything yet. After sharing a few pleasantries and explaining what our group was up to, I paid up, we said our goodbyes, and I clomped back out of the bar, a bit unsteadier in my bike shoes than when I arrived.

I walked my bike across the street where the rest of the riders were lunching, curious as to why no one else had ventured into the saloon. Soon I would realize that not only did no one else have the same pre-trip vision or reason for coming on the trek that I did, but that they were smart enough not to get wasted while we still had fifty miles of cycling to go.

But for now, I was in great spirits. I grabbed a sandwich and had a pleasant ride for the next fifty miles as I imagined that I was riding the prairie on my faithful steed. I took my time in the reverie and was the last rider to camp. As I pulled into camp, where tents were already erected and fires started, I galloped my bike-steed into the middle of camp, pulled hard on the brakes, and in a cloud of dust, sat back and raised my front wheel, my faithful steed rearing up on its hind legs, lusty and excited after its hard ride.

* * *

Our campsite that night was just outside of Libby, Montana. The next morning, we were all famished. Since we had not eaten restaurant food for several days, we decided to refuel with breakfast at the Venture Inn, a local restaurant and lodging place.

The place was packed with early morning breakfasters. On the walls hung dozens of signed photographs of Meryl Streep and Kevin Bacon, residents of Libby while they shot *The River Wild*. While I was considering the six degrees of Kevin Bacon, I had the odd sensation that I was still in a movie – that Kevin and Meryl and I were actually stars in a larger movie, where I played the character actor in the bar scene, and now it was time for the breakfast scene.

While I was lost in my return to movie fantasy, my

friends managed to arrange a table for twelve. Most of the group were vegetarians, and they were struggling to figure out what they would eat on this reasonably remote Montana menu. I was mostly vegetarian at the time, but when I saw chicken fried steak with biscuits and gravy, I no longer needed to pore over the menu. Chicken fried steak it would be.

When I was a small fry in Fort Worth, Texas, our family never went out to eat, except on the birthdays of me and my sister. We got to pick where we wanted to eat and what we wanted. I have no idea how it started, but for a few years my pick was the Blue Star Inn, a Chinese restaurant, where I would order chicken fried steak with gravy and egg foo young. It was predictably delicious, and I've spent most of my life trying to find a chicken fried steak that could match the taste and textural bliss of those dinners at the Blue Star Inn.

Now there's chicken fried steak, and there's chicken fried steak, ranging from unappealingly tough to deliciously tender. The Venture Inn in Libby, Montana, did not disappoint. When they came with everyone's food, small platters of something or other that didn't contain meat were brought to all my friends. I was served a huge platter of chicken fried streak with biscuits and gravy. They laughed as they noted my indulgence, but I am pretty sure I saw envy in all their eyes, not because they wanted the meat, but because I had the largest serving of all.

And so, at our post-movie celebration breakfast, that last day on the set, Meryl and Kevin and I had a grand time reliving the Dirty Shame saloon scene, and my part in the bigger story. I recall nothing of the rest of the trip, being impossibly mundane compared to my moment of Montana cinema fame, finding my place in Big Sky country as a star in my own movie.

> *There's no business like show business*
> *Like no business I know*
> *Everything about it is appealing*
> *Everything the traffic will allow*
> *Nowhere can you get that happy feeling*
> *When you are stealing that extra bow*
>
> *There's no people like show people*
> *They smile when they are low*
> *Yesterday they told you, you would not go far*
> *That night you open and there you are*
> *Next day on your dressing room they've hung a star*
> *Let's go on with the show!*
>
> —BY IRVING BERLIN AND SUNG BY ETHEL
> MERMAN IN *ANNIE GET YOUR GUN*:

Music to My Ears

I can forget myself in music. It's a welcome rest from the decision-making angst of internal dialog. Music is a language, that can be expressive without words. When listening to people speaking a beautiful language that I can't translate, the meaningless sounds offer the same structural beauty of the sound of music: crescendos and decrescendos; major and minor keys with their respective emotions; interesting tonal progressions; staccatos and legatos; thundering fullness and exquisite sweetness, softness, and silence.

I am grateful my mother sensed my love of music early on, and encouraged song, piano, dance and the subsequent laying down of permanent neural circuits. The piano skills I began to learn at age five years remain at seventy. Although my singing career peaked as a pre-school torch-song singer, I still love to sing those 1950s love songs. I am quite sure on my deathbed I will still be able to sing and enjoy *Put Your Arms Around Me Honey, Hold me Tight*.

Church singing was different. In the pews, I always shared a hymnal with my father, who was possibly the worst singer ever born. I remember being unable to imagine how he could be so off-key. I couldn't even try to sing that poorly. My singing genes did not come from my father.

It was in church that I learned the pleasures of singing in

a choir, with its mix of male and female voices from bass to soprano. Solo work could be anxiety-producing, but singing in the choir was pure pleasure.

During a church service, singing in the balcony with the youth choir seemed unimpactful, as the church was so large that our tiny and unsure voices were lost in the cavernous sanctuary. During choir practice, on the other hand, we were in a smaller room with great acoustics. The music director worked closely with us, letting us know how to blend our voices, to modulate volume, and to practice over and over until we got it. It was a great group experience, and helped me begin to understand that musical excellence required work, patience, practice, and confidence. I loved the moment at the end of a dynamic piece when the director would signal for us to stop singing, letting the sound of the mixed voices travel into silence.

The church music director had a love of "summer stock," and every summer would stage a musical that was appropriate for churchgoers. I enjoyed being in the chorus of HMS Pinafore. *"Let's give three cheers and one cheer more for the hearty captain of the Pinafore."* And why does this Pinafore earworm persist for me? *"Raif. Raif Rackstraw. Raif, that name. Remorse, remorse."* It was wonderful to be part of a larger production that is practiced, and performed, for the delight of one's self, and for others.

⁂ * ✳

I WAS INTRODUCED TO ANOTHER FORM OF GROUP SING-ing my first year in college, when Peter, Paul, and Mary sang at the University of Virginia gymnasium, at that time a small venue not much larger than an old high school gym. They invited the crowd to sing along with *Puff the Magic*

Dragon, and then the refrain in the Dylan protest song, *"The answer my friend, is blowing in the wind…"* I was filled with the significance of song with political context, in this case pointing out the absurdities of war and inequality. The power of this participatory singing event made me feel more mature, and filled me with the sense that there was work to be done in the world, and that I and this singing crowd of contemporaries could make the world a better place.

My most powerful group singing experience was in 1969, at the March on Washington, to protest the Vietnam War. On a cold day in November, I joined with a half million people marching through the streets of Washington, D.C. The crowd ended up on the grounds of the Washington Monument, where George McGovern, Gene McCarthy, and others spoke through loudspeakers from a central stage. The murmuring and conversations of the throng made the political rhetoric distant and inaudible. We knew what we were there for, although outside of marching and making our presence known, we weren't sure what to do next.

When Pete Seeger mounted the stage, he began singing the John Lennon chorus, *"All we are saying, is give peace a chance."* A half million people, for as far as you could see in all directions, joined in singing this simple phrase, over and over and over; the epitome of peaceful protest. And then Seeger started shouting, shaking his fist at the White House visible through the trees, "Can you hear that, Nixon! Can you hear that?" The crowd turned up the volume in determination. The emotion was chilling, making my scalp tingle, as it does to this day when I bring that memory from its hiding place, deep within. With song, a determined crowd helped stop a senseless and bloody war.

Then there was rock and roll.

In college in the 60s, music was to be heard everywhere. It was a golden age of musical creativity and freedom of expression. We danced to the beat of the Doors, Stones, and Four Tops, attended live concerts, and gathered to listen to the latest LP albums.

When Janis Joplin came to town, the arena was packed. She was really bringing it, when some drunk Wahoos down front started yelling, distracting from the beautifully quiet parts of her soulful *Ball and Chain*. At a natural song break, she stopped singing and began berating the drunks in a several minutes-long tirade. The flow of her words was as powerful as the song, delivered on a single note, as if part of the song. As she finished her say, she gave the band the sign to pick up where they left off, and without missing a beat, returned to *Ball and Chain* with Janis wailing the bridge, as only she could, "*…I said whoa, whoa, whoa, …*" The crowd exploded in appreciation, as we thought the song was over and expected Janis to storm off the stage. It was a masterful performance.

My college roommate Louie Nigro was an ancient Italian history major from Long Island who introduced me to the gastronomic delight of authentic multi-course Italian dinners served by his mother. I introduced him to Southern fried chicken, served by my mother. We hung out together and got in trouble together. After college, Louie taught for a while, then inexplicably became the US Ambassador to Chad.

The University of Virginia was a men's school at the time, and had "big weekends" ever so often, with women flowing into Charlottesville for a good time – parties, dancing, and plenty of drinking, which started on Thursday night and lasted through Sunday afternoon. I often think how lucky I was to survive that time. Several of my college mates did not.

Louie lost all inhibitions when he had too much to drink. One weekend, the Four Tops came to town, and we were all crammed into the fieldhouse to see a great show. The crowd was drunkenly raucous, and the Tops had the place jumping. This was Louie's favorite group, and at parties, when the dance bands would play Four Tops songs, Louie always headed to the mike to be lead singer. The local bands got to know him after a while and let him do it. He was a pretty good singer, and watching him sing was fun for all.

This night, as the Four Tops were winding up their charged show with, *"Reach Out I'll Be There,"* I was amazed to see Louie, who I thought had been sitting right next to me, get up on the stage, walk over to where the Four Tops were engaged in their characteristic line dance, and start singing with them, *"I'll be there, with the love that will shelter youuuu."* Amused, they let him sing and dance with them in their spectacular finale.

Now if you feel that you can't go on
Because all of your hope is gone,
And your life is filled with much confusion
Until happiness is just an illusion,
And your world around is crumblin' down;

Darling, reach out
Reach out (reach out for me.)

I'll be there, with a love that will shelter you.

I'll be there, with a love that will see you through.

When you feel lost and about to give up
'Cause your best just ain't good enough
And you feel the world has grown cold,
And you're drifting out all on your own,
And you need a hand to hold:

Darling, reach out
Reach out (reach out for me.)
I'll be there, to love and comfort you,
And I'll be there, to cherish and care for you......

Louie Nigro, the Fifth Top, future US Ambassador, may he rest in peace.

* * *

DURING MY EARLY YEARS AS A DOCTOR, EUGENE'S FREE clinic had a service known as Rock Medicine. Whenever a rock and roll group came to Eugene, whichever volunteer doc was on call for Rock Medicine would manage any medical problems the rock group needed, and in return got a backstage pass to the show.

The Grateful Dead liked to come to Eugene to visit the Keseys, and at the first opportunity I made sure I was the Rock Medicine doc. On the day of the show, my scheduler came up to me excitedly and said, "Guess who your next patient is!" In walked Bob Weir, lead singer and rhythm guitar player for the Dead. Of all things, he had a sore throat, hours before showtime. I can't remember what I did for him, as the memories of peering deep into the place from whence great music emerged overwhelmed the memories of the pedestrian task of treatment. Whatever I did, it must have worked, as their show that night was spectacular.

Later, as I watched the Dead perform from side stage, lost in their music, swaying with my head and body to Jerry Garcia's solos and unique band rhythms, a soft voice behind me said, "They can really play, can't they?" I turned my head to see Ken Kesey. "You got that right," I smiled. Here I was, onstage with Ken Kesey and the Grateful Dead. Such a night.

* * *

One summer we took Chagdud Tulku, a Tibetan Buddhism lama, to see the Dead in a special outdoor concert at the Country Fair grounds in Veneta. When our entourage arrived, the ushers, seeing the imposing figure of Chagdud in his traditional robes, motioned us to sit on the grass up front. Front row seats for the Grateful Dead! This was a good sign.

During the intermission, a roadie came out and said Jerry Garcia, the heart and soul of the Dead, was requesting the pleasure of Chagdud's company. Chagdud looked at me worriedly. I gave a slight nod and look that communicated, "Of course! Yes! Yes!" Chagdud agreed and insisted I come along. We were led back to an old yellow school bus, where the black-bearded and long-haired Jerry Garcia sat mid-bus with his guitar. He softly told Chagdud he would like to play him a song. Chagdud nodded, and there, in a school bus in the country, East met West, as Jerry Garcia played a quiet and beautiful song for Chagdud. I was overwhelmed by the generosity and thoughtfulness of Garcia, by the smiling engagement of Chagdud, and by the deeply expressive language of music. It was a song I had never heard before, or since. It seemed to be a special composition for a special moment.

* * *

FALLING IN LOVE WITH JANE WAS THE HAPPIEST TIME OF my life. There always seemed to be a musical accompaniment to our romance. I wrote songs for her during the courtship, sang, and played piano for her. During that time, I played the best classical piano of my life, focusing on the romantic and majestic complexity of my favorites, Chopin and Liszt. Music filled me, as I'm sure it filled Chopin when he wrote his love songs to lady friends. I loved feeling that I was in the mind of Chopin. To hear his music played is divine; to play it is rapturous. The music played itself through my hands and fingers. I was not in control; beautiful music just emerged. I was just the vessel, a vessel in love.

One of the many reasons I fell in love with Jane was her ability to play guitar and sing. When she gave me a private performance of her favorite Joni Mitchell songs, I couldn't believe how lucky I was.

Jane was ten years younger than I and had grown up listening to a different decade of contemporary music. As we compared notes on our favorite singers and groups, I was disappointed to hear she did not care for the Grateful Dead. She explained that when she worked at the Berkeley Women's Health Care Collective, the Dead often played nearby. She had heard too much Dead, and was no longer interested in them.

I couldn't believe it, but knowing she was a folkie, and a fan of acoustic, unproduced music, I asked if she would listen to the great Robert Hunter/Jerry Garcia song *Ripple*. As I cued it up on the turntable, I thought, this will be a real test of our relationship. We listened, and as the final strains drifted through the air, she looked at me after a perfect pause and said, "Now that's a good song." I always tear up recalling that sweet musical moment.

* * *

WHEN IT COMES TO CREATING MUSIC, AS OPPOSED TO passive enjoyment, I always return to the first instrument I learned how to play, one that I've had my entire life: my voice. I was born to sing, and it seems logical to go out singing.

I've karaoked twice in my life: once in a Elks Club dive bar in Longview, Washington; the other in a large beer hall in Grants Pass, Oregon. Both times I was on business with crazy Larry Abramson. He could not pass up any opportunity to visit a karaoke bar, and if you were travelling with him, you could be assured what one of the stops would be. Larry was so enthralled with karaoke that when he left town for another job, he threw a party for himself, rented a bar, and sang three sets of karaoke music, dressing differently for each set, to the bewilderment of the invitation-only crowd.

The challenge in karaoke is finding the right song. At the Elk's Club, it was the Mel Tillis/Bobby Bare version of *Detroit City,* a song that has stuck in my mind since I first heard it as a teenager. I loved its plaintive chorus,

> *"I wanna go home;*
> *I wanna go home:*
> *oh, how I want to go home."*

It starts out, *"Last night I spent the night in De-troit City."* Of course, I changed it to *"Last night I spent the night in Long-view City,"* which was the truth. Apparently, my version brought down the house for the dozen or so bar patrons. At a karaoke break, the jukebox sent everyone to the dance floor. A woman who had clearly lived a hard life of cigarettes, coffee, and alcohol, who could have been anywhere between thirty-five and fifty-five years old, sidled up to me on the dance floor and asked, "Are you married?" "No," I said, then quickly said, "I mean, yes." She looked at me, pushed me in the chest, and said, "Well make up your mind!"

My second and so far last karaoke experience was following a Rogue River raft trip, when we stopped in Grants Pass to refuel on beer and food. The bar was massive, and there must have been a hundred people there that night. I finally figured out my song, and when it was my turn, I have to say, I sang a great version of the Stones' *"Time...is on my side."*

After I nailed the finish, I looked over at the DJ, who mouthed earnestly, "Great job." Then I looked out at the audience, where the 100 people all had their cigarette lighters flaming high in the air, in comic tribute. It was, no doubt, the best, and most appreciated performance of my life.

And so, as I age out of the spotlight and ponder what to do with my remaining time, I have an idea of what I might do next. I started out as a singer in my mother's kitchen, singing with the radio before I could even remember, so it would give my life symmetry to end it as a singer. A new career awaits. I'm thinking sidewalk karaoke.

Immaculate Conception

I have always had a soft spot for salt of the earth folks afflicted by mental disorders beyond their choosing, notably schizophrenia and bipolar disorder. I had the privilege of meeting many of them after cuts in the county's mental health budget made it necessary for physician volunteers to manage psychiatric patients' routine medical concerns. As one of those physicians, I wouldn't have to manage the schizophrenia, or the bipolar disorder. I was just the body mechanic, the body shop.

Pam was single and childless, a genuinely delightful and upbeat thirty-year-old, uneducated but intelligent in the ways of the world. Despite being incapable of working at a traditional job or having a significant relationship due to her unstable bipolar disorder, she made the most of her life. Her exuberance and complete absence of cynicism made her someone I was always happy to see on the day's schedule, as I knew it would most likely be an interesting, and not unimportantly relaxing break in the usual intensity of the day. She would simply ask for advice, unencumbered by any expectations as to the outcome of our visit. I would not have to negotiate preconceptions.

One day she came in, with this complaint headlining her chart: "Something is wrong with my nose." Chart complaints always need to be checked, as a game of telephone invariably mangles something in the chain of messages that occurs between the time someone calls the office to state why they want to be seen, and whatever appears on their chart as the reason for visit. After exchanging pleasantries with Pam, I started my usual clarification process with an open-ended, "What's going on?"?

On that day the chart's message was close to being right, only Pam posed it as a question—"*Is* there something wrong with my nose?" Ah, a world of difference between a statement and a question.

I asked her a few simple questions as to why she thought there might be something wrong with her nose. Have you noticed anything? Have you been sick? Does it hurt? Did someone say something about your nose?

All nos. It was as if we were playing Twenty Questions, and the answer would never be revealed. Perhaps there was no answer. I eventually saw this approach might take a while.

"OK", I smiled, "let me take a look." I knew Pam was comfortable with me, because I was easy with her. It was like it should be, two people having a conversation, trying mutually to figure something out. I looked closely and carefully at her nose and moved it around with my finger. I spelunked her dark nasal orifices with my nasal speculum and headlamp, being careful to be gentle. I could see her watching me closely, and feel her anticipation as I explored. I looked extensively for the slightest thing wrong and didn't see a thing.

"You nose looks fine to me."

Pam immediately began beaming, and effervesced, "Oh, thank you, Dr. Jefferson!"

And that was it. That was all she needed to know. We both smiled, and she was on her way, practically dancing out of the room in celebration that nothing was wrong with her nose. I thought how easy it was to make someone's day, and to be the in the sacred place of expertise, the incredibly powerful position of someone who knew, and could say with authority and conviction, what a normal nose looked like. All those hours and years of training were finally paying off, producing these simple, wonderful moments!

*   *   *

PAM'S BIPOLAR DISORDER WAS USUALLY REASONABLY managed with her medication, when she remembered to take it. But sometimes she forgot, and would start to feel really good, until everything stopped making sense, including herself. Once or twice a year, she lost touch with conventional reality and required hospitalization to stabilize.

One morning, while working in my office, I got a call from the local psychiatric unit. Pam had been admitted a day or two before, was being stabilized again, and was complaining of a vaginal discharge. Despite being freshly psychotic and facing a pelvic examination on a psych ward, she did have the presence of mind to request that I come in to do the exam. The question now was, "Is there something wrong with my vagina?" Or, as she would have likely said, if it had been her calling to make a visit rather than the psychiatric ward nurses, "I've got a problem where the sun don't shine."

The hospital was only a mile or so away, so I dropped by during my lunch break. She was predictably happy to see me, and we clasped hands while welcoming each other. We both knew the routine of gynecological exploration, and I proceeded with the exam, with two psychiatric nurses as chaperones.

I noticed right away that she did indeed have a foul-smelling vaginal discharge. As soon as the speculum contacted vulva, Pam began peppering me with questions on what I was finding. I kept a running commentary of my every move, to keep her occupied and reduce her anxiety, being careful not to rush the exam. "I'm still looking, I'm going a little further." When I finally had full visualization, I noticed what appeared to be a piece of paper deep inside her, perhaps part of a tampon? This was an interestingly common and embarrassing (for the examinee) finding during investigation of a vaginal discharge.

"There's something here, were you using a tampon?"

"No. What is it?"

"I can't tell yet."

I asked for forceps to grab hold of the paper and retrieve it. As I carefully removed it, Pam incessantly asked me,

"What is it? What is it?"

As I delivered the paper to the outside world, I saw that it was a depiction of Jesus lying in the manger, wrapped in swaddling clothes, a picture that had been scissored out of a magazine.

"It's a Baby Jesus."

There was a perfect amount of silence as Pam processed this news. Then, from my position between her legs, I heard a quiet…"Oooooooh…", a beautifully intonated "O", starting midrange in pitch, then falling smoothly, as she now understood.

But I didn't.

I rolled around to her side on my chrome-plated examination chair, so that our eyes were on the same level, and simply asked,

"What?"

Pam, still in the stirrups, the chaperones hovering quizzically, explained that she had been looking at a magazine and saw a picture of the Baby Jesus. She developed a longing so intense for him to be *her* baby that she cut out the picture and placed it deep into her vagina.

"I wanted the Baby Jesus to be in my womb."

"Ooooooooh….," I replied, as I now understood how this made a strange kind of sense. However, it was best not to dwell there too long, so to conclude the episode, and to be respectful, I hesitantly inquired,

"Do you still want Him?"

Thankfully, she declined the soggy and odorous icon, which was no longer what she had in mind, now that she was thinking a little more clearly. I carefully placed the Baby Jesus in the trashcan, ending his brief sojourn. I looked up at the two nurses huddled around this woman swaddled with blankets, me holding her hand, and for an instant visualized an odd diorama blending a nativity scene and the Last Supper.

OK, time to leave the psych ward.

I realized it was up to me to break the spell and return us all to conventional reality. "Well, that's what was causing your vaginal discharge. They'll give you something to help clear things up from here." Pam and I clasped hands again, smiling at each other, both grateful for this wonderful coming together that resolved in a chuckle for all, free from any judgment or embarrassment. "It was nice seeing you again, glad I was able to help out."

"Oh, thank you, Dr. Jefferson!"

In the middle of a busy day, I was called to deliver the Baby Jesus. It was one of the best lunch breaks ever.

Altered States

I was astride a large white horse, with no saddle. The horse's front legs were up, and we were falling backwards through an infinite black expanse. Magnificent music was playing, dominated by a full set of orchestral strings, like the long crescendo in Sgt. Pepper's *A Day in the Life*, but this was twenty years before that song was composed. Instead of the music expanding upward in tone, it expanded outward, without melody. Both the horse and I were relaxed, as if this were an everyday occurrence within the splendor of being. There was no terror of falling, only the wonderful sensation of it.

The falling faded, replaced by cartoonish Snow-White dwarves lined up on either side of my lower teeth. Each dwarf was a little over twice as tall as the teeth, standing in the gum recesses, picking at my teeth from alternate sides using dwarf-sized pickaxes, singing *Whistle While You Work* as accompaniment to their dental mining endeavor.

I waked to a smell, the smell of a gas mask that had been placed over my nose and mouth, just before the ether dreams started. Two teeth had been painlessly removed from the Tootsie Roll and Sugar Daddy-diseased architecture of my ten-year-old mouth, while I had been transported to this wonderful new world. I had been introduced to alternative reality, and I liked it.

∗　∗　∗

A year later, I suffered a concussion. I had been playing at Mike Taylor's house, and my mother came by to pick me up on her way to the grocery store. I have no memory of the event, but she said that as I ran down the flat driveway to get to the car I stumbled and fell, hitting my head on the concrete. I lay there, unmoving.

When I woke I was lying on a couch in a strange room, first seeing a ceiling. I looked around and saw unfamiliar bookcases; it appeared I was in a living room. The people around me were not yet in my awareness. I uttered the classic words, "Where am I?" Not exactly what my mother was hoping for, although she was relieved I was awake. It was as if I had awakened from sleep but had been transported into a dream.

My mother had carried me, unconscious and limp, into Mike Taylor's house and laid me on their living room couch. I had never been in their living room, which accounted for my momentary disorientation. I had been out for twenty minutes or so. After I regained my senses and seemed to be ok, I was taken home to rest – no trips to the doctor in those days. I was back to being me, but the strangeness of coming back to reality and not knowing where I was, lingered with me.

∗　∗　∗

One afternoon in college I took a nap in the bedroom of a house several of us had rented in the countryside outside Charlottesville, Virginia. It was summer. The sun was streaming through the open windows, everyone was gone, there was no noise except for the wind in the trees. Such a pleasant time for a nap.

I was awakened by someone tugging on my tongue by a long sinewy thread. I couldn't see who was pulling it, but it was relentless and uncomfortable. I was paralyzed, unable to move. I was on the verge of panic, as I was wide awake, yet trapped, with someone pulling on my tongue.

Being simultaneously awake and asleep, I was able to contemplate what to do. One way out was to scream, to emit a guttural yell to jolt myself awake. However, I was too paralyzed to scream; my tongue was "tied." I reasoned, since I was awake within a dream that had emerged from sleep, why not go back to sleep and start over? That is exactly what I did: I went back to sleep, never really having been awake in the first place. With some level of awareness I extricated myself from the self-generated dream of torture by tongue pulling.

Ever since that nap I have puzzled over it. *Why* was I dreaming about someone pulling my tongue while I was helpless? Why was I "tongue-tied?" Why did I become aware within a dream? What a wonder to wonder!

* * *

One of the "high" points of my life occurred at the Cherry Blossom Festival in Washington, D.C. When I was in college at University of Virginia, I fell in with New Yorkers Tommie and Billy, and Baltimore Dave. It was the 60s, and we were experimenting with grass and LSD, to the backdrop of the great sound tracks of the day. Billy had a line on some New York blotter acid, which we had tried a couple of times at "starter" doses. We would listen to music while waiting for the drug to take effect, then head out without a plan. I loved watching trees breathe, inanimate objects move, and the wonder of after-images. I enjoyed how reality could be seen differently.

We were interested in experimenting with a slightly higher dose and decided to take our trip on the road. We thought watching the cherry blossoms in bloom in D.C. would make for a great display. So off we went.

When we arrived, we ritually placed the paper acid square on our tongues ......and soon found that doing an intense dose of LSD with thousands of people milling around, with cherry blossoms riotous and sprinkling their petals everywhere, was too much. We all began to fragment, to wander in our own directions, trying to make personal sense of the chaos. I was overwhelmed and decided to lie down on the manicured grass near the Washington Monument and just observe the obelisk.

As I lay on my back, knees bent, legs spread, hands clasped behind my head, in a restful gazing mode, I noticed the Washington Monument was shooting up skyward from between my legs, like a giant white phallus. This amusement was all I needed to ground me, to narrow my attention from being engulfed and at sea, into a charmingly captivating and focused state of mind. It was not erotic in any way, but visually fantastic.

After a while Dave ambled up in his laid-back way, with his permanently bemused grin, and said, "Jefferson, what are you doing?" I told him, his grin broke through into a laugh, and he happily joined me in the phallic fantasy. It is forever painted in my mind, an image not likely to go away.

During my medical internship in Portland, a fellow intern broke both legs skiing on Mt. Hood, requiring surgery. When I asked him about it later, he looked me straight in the eye and told me emphatically, "If you ever need anesthesia, ask for ketamine." I logged this away as potentially useful information.

Years later I got my chance. One Friday evening while playing in a city league softball game, I broke my thumb in a collision at second base. At the ER I was told to come back in the morning for a surgical procedure to have a pin placed to stabilize the fracture.

There can be advantages in being a physician, as in this case I knew the orthopedist and the anesthesiologist well. The anesthesiologist offered a choice of general anesthesia, or a nerve block, which involved sticking a needle into my neck. I didn't want general anesthesia and told him I was afraid of the nerve block. Memorably, he told me he didn't blame me. He and his fellow doctors had practiced nerve blocks on each other in anesthesia school, and he relayed that to this day he still had numbness and tingling in his fingertips from the experience.

When I asked about ketamine, he looked at me quizzically and asked if I knew what to expect, especially on awakening from the anesthetic. Ketamine is chemically related to LSD. It is an extremely safe and effective general anesthetic, and is widely used in veterinary surgery, and sometimes in pediatric surgery. Anesthesiologists love it due to its low side-effect profile. The downside for adults is that you are essentially getting an anesthetic dose of LSD, so that when you wake up, you are under the influence of a hallucinogen. A hospital is not the greatest venue to experience visual and other experiential anomalies, and thus ketamine was rarely used for adult anesthesia.

From my experiences with LSD, I felt that I would be able to handle the effects. After all, I might find the equivalent of a Washington monument to keep me occupied! And so it was agreed to.

The surgery was memorable. Ketamine is nothing like the blackout of general anesthesia: I entered a dream world. As the anesthetic took effect, I was able to perceive, above my body lying on the operating table, a triangle of moving noise. I could not only hear, but *see* the noise. It was a fairly loud beelike noise, like a loud zipper travelling from point to point on the triangle—

zzzzippppp……..zzzzippppp…….zzzzzipppp….

This was quite vivid, and entertaining. (Later, I deduced that the three points of the triangle were the surgeon, the nurse, and the anesthesiologist, talking to each other, and I was tracking the movement of conversation from one to the other in the hallucinatory state. I could not distinguish words, just location and movement.)

Awakening brought the next phase of the drug effect. It was Saturday morning, and the recovery room was pleasantly quiet. Realizing where I was, I continued to doze on and off, trying to remain in the pleasurable ketamine dream world.

Too soon it was off to the ward. The charge nurse informed me that I would stay there until I could take fluids, eat something, and walk down the hall on my own accord. We'll see about that, I thought; the orthopedist had told me he left an order that I could leave when I was ready. He assumed that, as a physician, I would use good judgment.

As they wheeled me into my shared hospital room, my roommate was watching the Saturday baseball game of the week on TV. Great! Baseball! Could life get any better?

While the nurses began their routines, I tried to keep my focus on the TV. The reality of being in a hospital bed with a cast on my arm, the side rails of my bed up, nurses milling around, and overhead speakers paging doctors, was a bit too chaotic with a hallucinogen on board. As my anxiety mounted and I was thinking how foolish it had been to put myself in this position, Pete Rose hit an inside-the-park home run, one of the most exciting plays in baseball. With fascination, I watched as it took an eternity for him to round the bases. Pete was running as fast as he could, but in slow motion to my eyes, leaving a trail of Pete Roses behind him. Priceless! As he rounded the bases, I was yelling, Yes! Yes! Yes!

The nurse waited for my excitement to fade, then asked what I would like to eat and drink. "A hot dog and a beer! And some peanuts!" She glared at me and offered me Jell-O and 7-Up, curiously hyphenated offerings. I tried the 7-Up, thinking that would be safe, but after one sip, I found the taste strange and chemical. It was then I knew I had to get out of there. I knew I was ok, knew the doctor had said I could leave when I wanted to, so I told the nurse I was ready to leave.

She looked me firmly in the eye and said, "Not until you eat and drink something and walk down the hall on your own." The nurse had the doctor in bed with the guard rails up, and she was not going to compromise.

     As Fate Would Have It

I knew there was no way I could walk yet. I began to get rambunctious, and the nurse left, only to be replaced by a new presence by my bedside, a presence that was large, and hovering. They had summoned a nun to calm down the drug-crazed doctor. She just stood there, hands clasped, exuding peace. I looked at her habit and her serene face, then noticed the metallic Jesus on the cross above the door behind her. I figured I better play it cool. The fact is, I calmed down. The nun gambit had worked.

After the nun left, I developed a new plan requiring my wide-eyed, but patiently observing wife, as a co-conspirator. I waited until the charge nurse was on her lunch break, and when the relief nurse came in, I explained that there was an order on the chart that said I could leave when I was ready, and I was ready. She checked the chart, and said, ok, as if that settled that. I was wheelchaired down the hall to the elevator, out the door, and slid into the back seat of my wife's car. While she drove me home, I lay blissfully on the back seat, imagining that I had just been surreptitiously sprung from prison.

Once home, I plopped into bed and was immediately at peace. Compared to the chaos of a hospital, there is no place like home. I lay there for hours, drifting on and off in pleasant sleep, finally to awaken with the greatest hunger in my life, relieved with a special order of Poppi's kotta psiti to replenish my soul.

* * *

RECENTLY, I WAS WHEELED TO THE ER WITH AN OPEN fracture of my left upper arm, which had shattered into many pieces, requiring extensive cleaning and the surgical insertion of plates and screws. The entire episode of the falling, getting help, the ambulance ride and the wheeling into the ER had been quite traumatic, with both my present and my future now a mess. They had given me Fentanyl for pain, so I was reasonably comfortable—as comfortable as one can be lying in an ER trauma room with one arm hanging on only by skin, nerves, and arteries, with IVs going and people scurrying around.

It was a Friday; Fridays are when the weekend's trauma cases begin to stack up. The trauma surgeon came by, looked at my arm and the X-rays, and decided I was to be his last case of the day, as my surgery was going to take him a while (he was right—it took several hours). I would have to wait in the ER for five hours before my turn in the operating room. He talked it over with the ER doc, after which he came over, peered down at me on the stretcher, and told me that since it was going to be a while before they could get to me, they needed to try to pull the bones into place while I was waiting. I nodded my head, knowing this was proper procedure, and well aware this was going to hurt. Then the ER doc said, "I usually use ketamine for this." I am sure a smile came across my face as I said, "Great, I've had it before, I know what to expect, let's do it." I was past ready for Never Never Land. As the ketamine drifted in through the IV, I welcomed the now-familiar dream world returning.

This time the experience was beyond description. I knew something was happening, but it was all very fuzzy, perhaps due to the Fentanyl. Dreamy music was playing, enriched with harp glissandos. It was one of the most pleasurable experiences of my life, in the midst of one of the worst experiences of my life. I was in a very good place, immersed in the color and sound palette of beauty and peace. My body was broken; my mind had never been better.

As I began to emerge from bliss, I opened my eyes and saw a glaring overhead operating light and two technicians putting a temporary cast on my arm. "Oh," I said. "*This* reality." The technicians chuckled knowingly. I was still in the ER, still in a terribly traumatic situation, awaiting surgery. I would be in the hospital for a few days followed by a long period of rehabilitation. This was a shocking dose of reality, a letdown. But for a while I had once again visited the pleasure realm, oblivious to pain and its attendant trauma.

* * *

WITH THE PERSPECTIVE THAT TIME'S PASSAGE BESTOWS, I find it amusing to review some of the elements that have grounded me while in an altered state: cartoon or fantasy reality; experiencing a tree deeply; a giant phallus; a baseball game; a nun with her cross. I suppose these categories – fantasy, nature, the erotic, sports, religion—are not much different than those many people use to deal with the stresses of reality. I see now that I wasn't really grounded, which implies a firm, solid, reliable base of reality. In the midst of emerging chaos, it was the re-focus of my attention that brought relief. And when the doors of perception opened a little too widely, when the view became a touch too overwhelming, there were always these pathways, and always followed by.......Oh, *this* reality.

After the Fall

Early on, my mother said I was accident prone. Looking back, I won't disagree. Besides, you don't disagree with my mother.

My first trip to an emergency room came courtesy of Coca Cola. Being an average Fort Worth four-year-old, I was raised on Fritos and Coke. Coca Cola had a bottling company in Fort Worth, and Fritos were invented in San Antonio. We were pioneers in buying local corporate food.

One hot summer day, I was sitting in the back seat of our post war Pontiac, on the way back from Chikotsky's grocery store, minding my own business. On the floor was a six-pack of Coke, in those wonderful small greenish tinted bottles, with the city of bottling on the bottom. It was a special prize to find a Forth Worth bottle. I loved Coke.

The heat and the jostling pressure were apparently too much, and one of the Coke bottles exploded, a broken shard of glass cutting into my ankle. My mother wrapped my bleeding foot in a towel, and off to the emergency room we went. This was one of my first memories – the car, the blood, my frantic mother, and the wasted Coke.

* * *

Bicycles were the source of more than one accident. My first bike was a Christmas present. I was so excited,
an amazing red Schwinn, with a speedometer and odometer! This was my ticket to leave home, to be on my own, to
ride with the wind in my hair, to explore where no boy had
gone. I rode twenty miles that day, so said the odometer.
The last stretch was a thrilling downhill, on a neighborhood street I had never explored. As I neared the bottom,
I saw, too late, that the street dead-ended in a circle. I back-
pedaled hard to brake, only to slide and crash into the curb.
That was the end of the day for me, and for my Christmas
present. Although I escaped with only scrapes, it was my
first lesson in how unforgiving and painful the effects of
gravity could be at high speed.

Despite this, I was allowed another bike. One of the
great pleasures of childhood came in summer, when the
DDT fogging trucks came to spray for mosquitoes. The
trucks put out dense clouds of white fog, and as soon as
the trucks hit the neighborhood, echelons of kids hit their
bikes to ride behind the trucks and within the cloud. It was
as if we were flying. We could barely see each other. What
great fun!

That is, until one ride, when I swung wide and ran into
a unseen car in the cloud, flipping me off my bike and over
the back of the car onto someone's lawn. The driver, morti-
fied, called my parents, who came to get me. It turned out
I was ok, but another bike was ruined.

✳ ✳ ✳

Animals made their contributions to my list of
injuries. I had a dog, Prissy, assigned to me, as children
were apparently supposed to have dogs. I would frequently

After the Fall   133

implore her to lick my ear when I needed a good feeling. I would say, "Prissy, bite my ear." The pleasure that followed was exquisite.

One day, as Prissy was nearing the end of her life, I was lying on my bed, bummed out about something, and Prissy walked in. A friend to console me! I leaned over the edge of the bed and instructed her, "Prissy, bite my ear!" This time she did. Bite my ear that is. Blood was everywhere, and I was off to the ER once again. I remember lying on my side with a paper sterile field over my head and a cutout for my ear, with a hot bright light above. During the suturing of the laceration, I could see an arc of blood slowly oozing cross the thin paper, a mesmerizing view of my exuding body fluids. I could hear the squeaking of the sutures as my ear was sewn up but couldn't feel anything due to the anesthesia. Prissy got put down soon after; it turned out she had cancer and must have had enough of me in her last crotchety days and took my instructions seriously.

I could go on, but you can see how my mother might have labeled me accident prone. Childhood was just the warmup. The pattern of gravitational wake-up calls did not change with aging. Two broken clavicles, two broken thumbs, dislocated fingers, a ruptured Achilles, concussions, a thoracic outlet injury, …. I just couldn't seem to stay out of the ER and OR. But the last catastrophic fall was a doozie, just a few years ago, when I was well into my sixties. I hope it's the last but, given my history, I can't count on it.

* * *

It was a beautiful but cold December day, the perfect day for a recently retired guy to be outside after weeks of miserable cold rain. The long-procrastinated roof moss project rose to the top of the to-do list. Trepidation triggered by ladders and steep wet shingles heightened the sense of dangerous adventure.

Access to my mossy roof was via an eight-foot lower roof edge from a back deck. Placing the ladder against the gutter, I began to climb. Everything felt solid, until that last fateful step from ladder to roof.

I had neglected to block the bottom of the ladder on the slick wooden deck. As I swung my leg up to the roof, the ladder slipped and fell away, and I was quickly headed to a crash on hard wood from eight feet. I had enough time to stretch my left arm out to break my fall, then crashed to the deck, ultimately lying face up.

As I lay there, momentarily pain-free from the massive adrenaline rush, I began to take stock of my status. I looked to my left and saw my arm lying on the deck, as if it had been broken off and tossed by my side. My first thought was that I had completely severed the arm. I screwed up the courage to try to wiggle my fingers, to determine whether it was still attached. Seeing my fingers wiggle was a tremendous relief.

I tried to get up, but my left hip balked. Oh no, I thought, a broken hip. This was not good. I lived alone and had left my cell phone on the dining room table. I lay there, contemplating my next move.

⋆ ⋆ ⋆

My mind wandered to an event in my mother's life. After us kids had left home and my father had died, she lived alone for a long time, in a house in Virginia with a large yard. She loved to garden; pulling weeds helped with her frustrations. She spent hours in her flower garden, assuring the flowers were perfect for making arrangements for her church, and for the Jimmy Carter White House. Weekly, for a while, an aide from the White House would come to her house to pick flowers to display there. She was very proud of her garden, and where it took her, and her flowers.

She loved that garden, but she was passionate about her fish pond. She talked to the few goldfish she kept there, and to the frogs that settled there. They were great friends for several years, my mother and the frogs and the goldfish. They relieved her loneliness in a way that flowers could not. She loved how those creatures could survive the cold and snowy Virginia winters, just like her perennials. Each spring, she waited to see if her friends would return.

One sunny and cold February day, when the goldfish and frogs were dormant, she went out to clean the leaves from the pond. She had become more frail in those days, and as she scooped the leaves with her net, she slipped on the mossy side of the pool, and fell in.

The pond was about three feet deep, and she was slightly less than five feet tall. In the middle of the pond was a large concrete fountain. As she fell, she hit her knee on the fountain and broke her leg. There she was, eighty-five years old, in a frigid pond in February, with a broken leg, living alone.

There were neighbors who lived close enough to hear her, so she called for help. But it was February and everyone's windows were closed, so no one heard her. Realizing this after a while, she knew it was up to her to get out of the pond. As she tells the story, she said, in a determined flourish, "Lord, if you want me to live, help me out of this pond." She grabbed the side of the pond and miraculously launched herself onto the surrounding grass.

She lay beside the pool, drenched, cold, and unable to get up. After a few more failed attempts at yelling for help, she knew what she had to do: she crawled the hundred feet to the front yard, dragging her broken leg. Once she got to the street in front of the house, she figured she could flag down a passerby for help.

That is exactly what happened. After the 911 call and the subsequent hospitalization and surgery, my mother was able to return to her garden a few months later. She loved to tell that story, as she had finally looked fate in the face and survived, as her namesake great grandmother Martha had done during the Civil War. Family lore has it that Martha brandished a hot poker at ransacking enemy soldiers, telling them to get out of her house, warning them that she meant business, and that "she would rather die in a hot fever than a slow death." At the age of eighty-five, my mother had lived up to the ferocity of her lineage and earned the wide-eyed respect of everyone who heard her story.

* * *

THIS STORY FLASHED THROUGH MY MIND, AS IT NOW WAS I who lay on my back on a deck on a cold December day, with a broken arm and hip. Now I knew what I had to do: call for help, and if that failed, crawl to the front yard.

I began my plea with a moderately toned "Help." When no help came, I modified my plea to a louder and louder "Help me," then back to "Help! "as the extra syllable seemed a waste of what breath I had left. As my pleas disappeared unanswered, I again changed my request, hoping that more clarification might help. Perhaps someone had heard, but was wary, and needed additional information to make sure it was not a hoax. "Help me, I can't move, I broke my arm and hip, I need help." I strained to hear a response, worried that my failing hearing might miss a reply.

I had no way to tell how much time passed, but eventually I had to admit it was now time for the next step, that of crawling to the front yard, something I was not looking forward to doing with a broken hip, and an arm that seemed connected only by flesh, and not by bone. But this seemed to be the family fate, so I tried to move, wondering how I was going to make it down a couple of steps and through a gate. But I found I was immobile with my broken left arm and hip. I couldn't move; I was not able to follow my mother's path. It was beginning to get cold in the December air. Is this the way it's going to end? No, too early for that.

I once again changed my request. "Help me. Call 911. I need help. I can't move."

After I had repeated this a number of times, I heard a faint, "Where are you?" A woman's voice. I couldn't tell from where.

"Call 911. I fell from a ladder and can't move. Call 911."

I waited. A while later, her faint but beautiful voice asked, "What's your address?" Aha, the piece of information the ambulance needed to find me. I now knew help would be on the way.

As it turned out, on this cold December day, a Korean woman who lived on the next street over and down a few houses, had company and a room full of wild children. She told me she never went outside on her deck this time of year, but to get away from the chaos, she had stepped outside for some peace of mind. It was then that she heard my far away cries for help.

The ambulance arrived, and the EMTs got to work. As they cut off my clothes, they found bones sticking out of my upper arm, splintered into many pieces and lying askew, revealing why it appeared from my supine vantage point that my arm was just lying there, not really belonging to me. When I heard their groans, I was glad I couldn't see what they saw. As they lifted me onto the gurney, one of them scanned the deck in the event something had been left behind and asked, "Is that a dog bone?"

"I don't have a dog."

It was a chunk of my bone they had found. They dutifully wrapped it in gauze, and the fragment accompanied me to the hospital. It could not be used in the subsequent repair, but despite the situation I was in, I found this an amusing part of the narrative, both then and now. EMTs say the darndest things. My amusement may have been assisted by the Fentanyl they gave me, as I had not suffered a head injury and they were allowed to give me some much-needed narcosis for the transfer.

As I lay in the ambulance, sirens blaring, Fentanyl on board, I remembered the last time gravity had taken its toll, and I had waited for an ambulance.

*　*　*

A DOZEN YEARS EARLIER, MY WIFE JANE AND I WERE about seventy miles into a ninety-mile bike ride, in a remote area of Buck Creek Road outside Lorane, Oregon, that was populated by bear and cougar. I was coasting downhill, tired, relieved not to be pedaling, and wishing the ride was over. The relief didn't last long. A surprise curve required braking and deciding which angle to take to take, at thirty miles per hour.

Loose gravel decided my fate. As I braked my rear wheel fishtailed in the gravel, and I went down. The left side of my chest fell on the handlebars, and I ended up in a heap with the bicycle, my breath taken away, gasping in agonizing pain.

Jane was following me and rode up to assess and help. I could feel that I had a broken rib, and worse yet, my bent wheels were not ridable. We were ten miles from the nearest house. Jane would have to ride for help, leaving me alone on the road.

I was stunned and in pain when she left. I had hit my head; my helmet was cracked. I found a position that lessened the pain, sitting on the road and leaning on one arm away from the chest pain. For an hour I was alone in the wilderness, not knowing what would happen. It is often unfortunate to be a doctor. This was one of those times, as I knew a high impact chest injury can tear arteries, causing one to bleed out internally. I had seen this very thing happen. A few years earlier, while driving home in a similarly remote area, filled with the wonder of observing steelhead leap upstream, I noticed a group of motorcycles pulled off the road, and a man doing one-person CPR by the side of the road. A motorcyclist had similarly hit some gravel and gone off the road, and unfortunately hit a tree. I stopped to help, and we quickly determined we had a first-class team doing CPR – he was an ICU nurse, and I was an emergency room physician at the time. We attempted resuscitation, but after a while it was clear that we would not be successful and terminated our efforts. The autopsy showed he had ruptured an artery in his chest and bled out quickly. There was nothing we could have done to save his life.

Sitting alone on Buck Creek Road, I reflected whether it was my turn to bleed out. I imagined I would be fine prey for a bear, or a cougar, or perhaps the turkey vultures I saw circling overhead. There was really nothing I could do but wait and try to clear my mind of worst-case scenarios.

     As Fate Would Have It

I entered a dream-like state of calmness and prepared to drift into oblivion. There was total silence; I was in a state of disembodied, timeless reverie. I was one with the woods, a wounded animal, waiting.

The arrival of my wife and an ambulance brought me back to reality. She had ridden the ten miles to the nearest house and called the local fire department. They assisted me into the back of the ambulance, and I knew I would be ok.

In the ambulance, I couldn't lie down and could only find comfort sitting up. As I had hit my head, they were not allowed to give me pain medication, so I had to endure what was quickly becoming increasingly lancinating pain with every pothole we hit. I began to fear this was more than a broken rib. I knew we were forty-five minutes from the emergency room, and the pain was becoming unbearable.

I asked the paramedics if they had ice to apply. No ice. I suggested they stop at the Lorane country store. Hilariously, that is exactly what we did. Imagine, an ambulance stopping for ice. That helped, but the next twenty miles were twenty of the longest miles of my life. I was never so grateful to arrive at the ER.

Evaluation there showed that I had not broken a rib; I had broken six ribs in two places each, having what is known as a flail chest, with the ribs depressed into my chest. My lung had collapsed, and I had bled into my lung, requiring insertion of a chest tube, a nasogastric tube, finally some pain medication, and an overnight hospital stay. For the next two months, I could sleep only sitting in a chair, not being able to lie down. And I could sleep for only two hours at a time, which was as long as the narcotics relieved the pain. It was a long two months, and the first really low part of my life.

In the woods, I had been seriously injured. Yet, my most vivid memory of the entire experience was the hour or so I waited alone for help, not knowing what would come next, with only my imagination as company.

* * *

These memories emerged during the much shorter and smoother ambulance ride from my ladder fall. Here I was again, in another ambulance, riding to the hospital with a shattered arm and hip, sirens wailing, with the previous bike crash and ambulance ride drifting through my mind. Ambulance memories. This ambulance ride was pain free due to the Fentanyl, and we were only fifteen minutes from the hospital. The ER docs determined that beside the shattered arm, that I had a pelvic, not hip, fracture, and that is what kept me from retracing the path of my mother, crawling to the front yard for help. I was relieved it was my pelvis and not my hip.

I got to spend several days in the hospital, followed by a few days in a rehabilitation facility and a month in a wheelchair. I got to witness a nursing home from the patient side for the first time, and it reinforced my belief that this was not my preferred final resting place.

* * *

The good news is, I heal well. It never ceases to amaze me how bodies and bones heal themselves, without conscious instructions. And, with the help of contemporary expert medical care, it is now as if the fall never happened. After each of these accidents, falls, and lacerations, I was made whole, to fall again another day.

I am reminded how fortunate I am to live in this time of neighbors, friends, EMTs, hospitals, doctors, nurses, good Samaritans, and all those who help us recover from calamities. In a different time and place in the history of the world, and in many places now, if I had fallen instead, say, from a tree, or a cliff, I would have died of infection and immobility, alone with my crushed body, awaiting the last hours, cursing my fate, or trying to understand why, and why now. And finally drifting into the final sleep.

What gods repetitively pick me up and throw me down, as if to say, wake up! Or, take that! Is this an initiation? Are they testing me? Hardening me up? For what? Teaching me a lesson? What is the lesson? What is the meaning of it all?

That life is perilous? That life is precious? That our lives depend on others? That other's lives depend on us?

Yes.

But the greatest test was not physical pain.

The Thrill of Victory

Jane was despondent the morning after her first world championship triathlon, Ironman Hawaii. There is a predictable letdown after a big race, just from physical and emotional exhaustion, but this was different. Although she had trained for a year, she'd had a disappointing race. Now forty, she had dreamed of this race since she was twenty-four, when, on ABC's Wide World of Sports, she watched Julie Moss collapse fifteen feet from the finish of the 1982 Ironman Hawaii, then crawl across the finish line because she could no longer stand. She was about to win the women's race, then got passed as she was crawling. Julie Moss's determination to finish was memorable. Jane was inspired. She thought I want to do that. Years later, here she was, her dream incomplete in her mind, not because it wasn't a great experience, but because she didn't have her best race. She was timid on the swim, cautious on the bike, and she bonked on the run.

I was her handler. I trained with her, ate with her, encouraged her, travelled with her. My job was to double-check that she had everything packed for the trans-Pacific voyage, help take her bike apart for transport and reassembly in Hawaii, and on the morning of the race, to assure that all the logistical details were taken care of, whatever it took to reduce the stress of race day. That meant helping her on with her wetsuit for the two and a half mile swim; making sure her bike, fluids, shoes, and helmet were perfectly laid out for a time-saving transition to the 100-mile bicycle leg; driving around the bike course to strategic spots to encourage her; blowing her a kiss as she transitioned from the bike to set out for her four-hour marathon run; and helping out after the race in whatever way I could.

During Ironman Hawaii the Kona coast teems with thousands of the fittest people in the world. Beautiful bodies preen everywhere, soaking up the sun; the pale-skinned Oregonians and the perfectly tanned Californians. We had arrived a couple of days early to settle in, and we managed to find a remote beach away from the chaos, where Jane swam with the turtles and relaxed. But the day before the race, as the island's anxiety level ramped up, she wanted to acquaint herself with the swim start, where two thousand people would swim into the ocean in a staggered start, crawling over each other, a spectacle of water frothing with humanity returning to the sea. There was a small beach there, with hundreds of other triathletes taking in the start, and each other. That patch of sand is known as Dig-Me Beach, and it was indeed that. Jane had a swim in mind; I was happy observing the fascinating display of men and women in peak physical shape, wearing next to nothing, all laughing anxiously. There would be no laughing once the race started. Jane joined the crowd, slipped into the water with many others, and stroked out into the ocean along the marked course route. After a long while, she emerged from the water with her characteristic smile and told me of all the beautifully colored fish she had seen, swimming with her. She was psyched.

Jane came from a family of swimmers. A brother and sister were good enough to participate in Olympic swim trials; her brothers were water polo athletes. They all had the physique and genetics for swimming – a muscular middle widening into the powerful strength of chest, shoulders and upper arms, and a heart made for endurance. From the middle down, they had powerful legs for propulsion, and the characteristic family thunder-thighs. In Jane's case, these distinctive quads, toned by thousands of miles of training on the bike, were responsible for her cycling power. In training and racing, she never saw a hill she didn't like; she loved the rhythm of working hard on the hills. She had the perfect body, background, genetics, and determination for what was for her an eleven-hour race.

Jane was a good swimmer and an excellent cyclist and loved those parts of the race. She knew who she was then, completely in touch with her body. She was never a fan of the marathon; it was an ordeal to go out and run for four hours while already exhausted. Her goal, like many, was to try to get a lead on the competition in the swim and bike, then hold on in the marathon. But her ability to excel at two of the three legs made her a very good age-group competitor. This Ironman came at an auspicious time, as she had just turned forty and would now be the youngest in the competitive women's forty-to-forty-fve age group. This would be her best opportunity to enter a frenzy with similarly determined women in their early forties. It was to be the biggest athletic competition of her life. She couldn't wait.

* * *

When we met, Jane swam for fitness, getting up every day at 5 am, year-round, to head out for a group swim in an open-air heated pool. She especially loved swimming in the winter, in the dark early morning hours, beneath the moon, with steam rising from the water, then swim until the sun rose. I was a city league softball player and had started to run in the off season for fitness, to keep my aging legs in shape. As we fell in love, we started running together, and turned out to be well matched in distance running ability. It was easy and challenging to train together. We began entering local road races, and both competed well in our age groups, and against each other.

When her thoughts first turned to triathlon, Jane had never raced bicycles competitively. Cycling would be the final skill needed to try her hand in triathlon. We fell in with a bicycling group, some of whom were fellow triathletes, and trained in running and cycling together for years. As it turned out, and to her surprise, bicycling became her best, and favorite sport. She was a natural. Her tremendous endurance and cardiovascular engine, along with her thunder-thighs, with more than a touch of competitiveness, quickly resulted in her ability to regularly crush the boys on the hills around Eugene. She loved beating the boys, and they dubbed her Queen of the Mountains. Now being proficient and confident in all three sports, she was ready to enter short course triathlons, which led to the longer Olympic race, then half-ironman, then the ironman distance: two-and-a-half- mile swim, 112-mile bike ride, twenty-six-mile marathon. During this time, she had one goal in mind–to qualify for the mother of all Ironmans, the world championships in Hawaii.

* * *

During this time, I continued to play men's league softball. A group of us came together as a team, became great friends, and for years played in the city's Friday night league. We would end our week and head out to the softball fields, play a game, then get together for beers, celebration, and the endless rehash of the critical or interesting points of the game. It was primo guy time. For those of us who loved to play baseball, baseball is life, the best game there is, and we could talk about it endlessly. We had good teams, strong at every position, and did well in our league.

I was an outfielder and loved to play left field. Something about robbing the big hitters of their best shots was challenging and entertaining to me. Some of the peak experiences of my life involved pursuing a batted ball as it arced through the air and, without thinking, calculating the trajectory and path of the ball, to arrive at the ball in full sprint, or better still, to fly through the air at full extension to snag the ball. I had the speed to outrun the ball and track down flies that others could not get to. Easy fly balls—boring. Fielding ground ball singles – sigh. Challenging fly balls—it just doesn't get any better than that. For me, it was the ultimate athletic feat. Catching a ball on the dead run is a magical, satisfying moment.

If you play long enough, there will be memorable and varied individual plays – memorable because of the catch, and because of the situation. Game-winning plays. Going in for the ball to your left and right to snag sinking liners. Going back to left and right to outrun long fly balls. Diving to the left or right, extended fully horizontally, with the ball just catchable, and, as an added bonus if the ground is wet, catching the ball at full speed in a dive, then sliding exquisitely with the ball in your glove, the pleasure of the catch extended by the slide, giving you precious seconds of extra happiness as you exult in the satisfaction of the moment.

I would dream up various catches, and then, over time, got the opportunity to make them. To make dream catches, I needed the cooperation of the ball being hit in exactly the right place, at the exact right trajectory, and the exact right velocity. After years of playing, as if it was meant to be, I had made all my dream catches. All but one: the no-look catch.

*　*　*

One night it happened. I was playing center this time, in a tight game, runners on first and second, two out. The ball was hit hard on a line over my head. Balls hit right at you are the hardest to judge, as you can't get a stereoscopic view to instinctively calculate the optimal angle of pursuit. But I knew at the crack of the bat where I thought the ball was going to land. I turned my back to the plate and sprinted to that spot, while keeping the ball in sight from the corner of my eye in the event I needed to make an adjustment.

But I was right on the money, and in the end, still at full speed, there was only one way to make the catch. I had to take my eye off the ball at the last moment, and in a dead sprint, fly through the air directly toward the centerfield fence with my back to the plate, extend myself and my glove fully to where I thought the ball would land……and made the no-look catch.

I couldn't dream up any different great catches, so this turned out to be the Last Great Catch. There is an upside and a downside to making the greatest catch you have ever made. The upside is obvious; the downside is you know it will never get better than that. I had now accomplished everything I wanted to do in the game. Except for one thing: to play in a major championship game.

Of the teams I had been on, there were plenty of league and tournament championships, but I never had the opportunity to play in a city or state championship. By this time, I was in my forties, an increasingly injury-plagued time to be playing softball, and I could see that the end of my playing days was near. Besides, my wife and best friend was a triathlete, and while she loved baseball, she wasn't so attracted to the softball guy scene. She had her own way to achieve athletic exhilaration. Then one day, I was invited to play left field, and hit leadoff, on a Eugene team entered in the national over-forty softball championship, which was in Portland that year. Now this was something. My teammates and I would be playing for a national title, a once in a lifetime opportunity. My dream had come true in my forties, and I knew in advance this was likely to be My Last Tournament.

Our team was a rag-tag group, but good. We travelled to Portland with no hopes of doing anything other than having a good time. But, to our surprise, we won our first game, on a Friday night. That resulted in us being bracketed to play our next game against the previous year's national champions from Oakland, California, that was favored to win the title again this year. At 9 a.m. Saturday morning.

Our team was known to party, and we were so delirious celebrating our first game victory, that we got thoroughly wasted on beer and weed. We joked and laughed until late at night, all piled into the same motel room, with no worries that we would be playing the national champions the next day. We were invincible. Nothing could stop us now.

The next morning, we were all a bit hungover. In the best of circumstances, no one in baseball is on top of their game at 9 a.m. Our late-night antics did not provide us with anything close to the best of circumstances.

We were up first and went one-two-three, and that was as close as we got to the power boys from Oakland. We lost that game 9-0, and Oakland went on to win the national championship once more. But we had played the national champs and had our shot at the title. I had a terrible game and was disappointed. It seemed like a sad day in Mudville, and in tribute to my identification with Casey, in baseball's great epic poem, I was inspired to write some verses for our team's wintertime talent show. It started,

> *"We were tied in the first*
> *With the national champs…,"*

That, as it turned out, had to be good enough. After all, my dream had been to play in a national tournament. I hadn't actually dreamed of winning it.

All this talk of baseball is a long way of saying that I learned, by sticking with my passion of playing, and watching baseball, and other sports, that, no matter how adept you and others are, it is almost axiomatic that the first time you make it to a big-time playoff or athletic event, it is very difficult to win if you are playing someone, or a team, who has been there before. The corollary to this is that the next time you reach the playoffs, it is you who has the experience. This valuable lesson turned out to be useful in Hawaii.

*　*　*

I loved playing baseball because it made me feel good: I felt in my element, and knew it was a game where failure is common. Jane loved triathlon because, despite the long hours of training, it made her feel good. Until it didn't.

And so, that morning in the hotel room in Hawaii, where Jane felt let down, and disappointed, in her first appearance in an international championship, I knew what she was going through. It was time for the handler to handle. One thing I had learned as a physician was the power of encouragement, and the power of the moment. Without really thinking about it, I went to a place of familiarity and told her a story, which went something like this:

The first time a team goes to the World Series, they often don't win it, as they can't tune out the hoopla and expectation, and lose who they are. But then, the players vow to be back; they want to be back. The high of skill, excitement, and accomplishment doesn't go away. They keep at it, because they know, in a hundred ways, they could have done better. And, they belong there. It is their passion. It is worth failure to gain the experience of being there. They say, I'll be back; this is what I love to do.

My schmaltzy locker-room speech flowed from me effortlessly. I was her coach, her handler, her lover. To see her like this was breaking my heart. Her confidence was shaken, and I had never witnessed that. The speech was the best I could come up with, to express what I was really trying to say: Don't give up. You have the tools. And now you have the experience.

After I had said my piece, she looked at me lovingly, threw her arms around me, and in that moment, as we embraced, we both knew she would train for another year. She would be back. She knew she could do better. She would know how to focus, and not let her energy be drained by the anticipation of her first world championship, the plane ride to Hawaii, and the intimidation of the fittest people in the world strutting their stuff on Dig-Me beach.

* * *

SHE DID COME BACK THE NEXT YEAR, WITH CONFIDENCE, and had the race of her life. As she ran through the cheering mob near the finish line, she had that beautiful smile on her face, the smile of swimming with the fish. It did not matter to her in what place she had finished, because now, as a seasoned veteran, she knew she had prepared well, and performed well. I was touched that she would not let them take her official picture without her handler. In her mind it was a team victory.

She didn't want to stick around for the post-race hoopla, as she was tired and wanted to get off her feet, knowing the next day would bring muscles so sore she would not be able to climb steps, except backwards. It was off to get cleaned up and try to sleep.

It wasn't until the next morning that we found out just how well she had done. I looked up the results on a computer to find that Jane had finished tenth in the world in her age group. Tenth in the world! Tenth in the world! We jumped around the hotel room in merriment, completing a year that had started with an embrace born of despondency and ended in an embrace of happiness. In that moment, in that hotel room, we both knew, without saying, that this was her peak experience in triathlon. It was to be her Last Great Race. It was on to the next chapter of her life.

Jane and TJ at Ironman Hawaii

Marys Peak

For four years the ashes sat boxed in my closet. I couldn't bear to look at or think about them.

The first two years they occupied space, hidden away. In the third year I decided what to do with them. In the fourth year I carried out my plan.

Jane's life ended suddenly, and unexpectedly, on a Memorial Day bike ride, killed instantly as she was sucked under and run over by a fully loaded log truck. She and I were truly soul mates; it was as if we were two bodies with one mind. Losing Jane was doubly traumatic; I lost her, and part of myself. Four years later, on Memorial Day, I set out in my car for Marys Peak, with Jane's ashes riding shotgun.

She worked in Corvallis two or three days a week, and on her commute from Eugene she watched the mountain change from winter snowcaps to spring verdancy. Locally they say, when the snow is gone from Marys Peak, it's time to plant your tomatoes. Jane's saying was, when the snow is gone from Marys Peak, it's time to climb it on your bicycle.

Every year we would ride our bikes from Monroe to the top of Marys Peak, rest happily and fulfilled at the top, then descend and return to Monroe through Alsea's lightly travelled back roads. Every year she looked forward to that seventy-five-mile pilgrimage.

She was a great climber. She was known as Queen Jane by the local riders, as she could climb with the boys, and often finish ahead of them. She was the Queen of the Mountains.

I was not a climber. Jane and I would ride together on the flats, but when it came to the climb, we had an agreement—she would ride her own pace to the top, where she would wait for me. I hated climbing, mostly because I couldn't keep up with her, but to be with Jane, I had to climb. Once you find your rhythm, the feeling of effort gives way to a meditative timelessness. It was that rhythm that she climbed for.

Marys Peak was known as Chateemanwi, or "place of spiritual power," to the native Kalapuya tribe that legendarily used the land for spiritual quests. From the east side of the summit, snowmelt and precipitation flows into the Willamette and Columbia Rivers and on to the Pacific Ocean. From the west side water flows directly to the sea. Marys Peak was the perfect place to let Jane go, into the sky, to wash into the ocean, where she would endlessly recycle, until our earth was no more.

* * *

For many years, I was a practicing Buddhist. I learned the benefits of meditation, visualization, and mantra, how to see the world in a different way, the importance of intention toward one's self and others, the interdependence of aliveness, and that we are all one.

I was taught by Chagdud Tulku Rinpoche, a delightful Tibetan lama who became my spiritual mentor. In 1959, he escaped from Tibet by horseback. After teaching in Nepal for many years, he was invited to America. He was a wandering yogi and went where he was called. After he visited Eugene in the 1980s, I was among a group who requested that he stay and teach us what he knew. Travelers often endured great hardships to trek to Tibet to learn at the feet of such a person. We in Eugene had crossed paths with an authentic Tibetan nomadic yogi, from the wilds of Tibet, schooled in ancient traditions. Tibet had come to us. We pitched in to support Chagdud and his wife, and he began the process of introducing us to the true nature of reality.

Tibetan is a poetic and musical language, and to hear him teach in Tibetan was riveting, even without knowing what he was saying. He taught poetically, with layers of meaning, and translators would often break into tears at the beauty of his words, and the difficulty of translating them into English.

He was a Tulku; an incarnate, or recognized being. In Tibet, at the time of death of an accomplished and revered lama, it is believed there is a choice: you can dissolve or eject your remaining consciousness into the realm of pure reality, or you can intentionally return to the human realm to continue to help relieve the sufferings of mankind. Buddha's famous starting point was that suffering happens, and that the work of relieving suffering in our world is never done. It is considered to be the final and greatest act of compassion to visualize, in one's last breath, a fervent intent to return to the world of suffering in order to help others. Such dying lamas would leave clues as to where to look for their next life.

After a great lama dies with such intention, and after an appropriate length of time, allowing for the birth and upbringing of a special child, a committee of spiritual scholars sets out on a trek to the designated area to find the reincarnate being. When the lamas come to a village, local families line up to determine if their child is the sought-after tulku. A series of tests are performed by the scholars, and the child's reactions determine whether they have the characteristics of the sought-after realized being. It is considered a great honor to have your child selected, even though it means that the child, at the age of five, will be taken to lama school, where they will study and immerse themselves in Buddhist philosophy and principles until they are twenty-one.

Chagdud was such a child. I saw his natural sense of presence, calmness, generosity, humor, lack of ego, and way of knowing. You could never beat him at a game of chance, where he would just laugh as you tried to outwit him. The first time he left Eugene, a group of twenty of us sat in a circle on the ground with him at the Amtrak station, sad that he was leaving. We were quiet, no one really knowing what to say, engulfed with the loss of his leaving, even though it was temporary. A woman broke the silence by asking, "Rinpoche, that sparrow that we rescued isn't doing too well. What do we do if it dies?" The lama from remote Tibet looked at her, contemplated for a moment, looked at all the sad faces, and with perfect timing, said, "Eat it!" with a belly laugh that immediately transformed our seriousness into a warm feeling of togetherness, and brightened the parting.

Not long after Chagdud came to America, it was arranged for him to meet with the Hopi spiritual leader in Arizona. Native Americans were originally nomads, believed to be wanderers from the region of the Tibetan plateau. Tibetan and Hopi people are similarly known for their spirituality and tradition of peace. Neither of them

     As Fate Would Have It

knew quite what to expect, and neither knew much if anything about the other's people. Later, Chagdud remarked, that when he entered the meeting room, he and the Hopi holy man locked eyes and immediately recognized that they were spiritual and racial kin, and tearfully embraced as if long-lost brothers.

And so in Eugene we had the incredible opportunity to learn the wisdom of a lineage that had considered and written about their take on the true nature of reality, for hundreds and thousands of years. Chagdud taught us the preliminaries of Buddhism, methods of purification, cutting through obstacles and negativity, the calming and training of mind, how to allow compassion and joy to emerge, and how to manage the difficulties of birth, sickness, old age, and death. On each full moon, we would practice what to do when we died. We learned how to help others as they were dying, and how to hold them in our thoughts in the time after death. We learned to inhale a troubled person's suffering and fill them with compassion as we exhaled. We sat for hours and days to watch our minds and learned that our entire experience is nothing more than our mind at work. We learned that we are always in a state of flux or change, that emotions can be like passing clouds or storms, and to not get too caught up in the storyline.

In addition to his education as a Tibetan lama, Chagdud was trained as a physician. He agreed to assess some of my patients that Western medicine had no answers for. He used pulse diagnosis, and observation of urine. He enjoyed being able to practice his skills, and the patients enjoyed his calm manner and methods.

One patient in particular had been diagnosed by "modern" medicine with "sero-negative polyarthropathy," which was a fluffed-up way of saying that she had migratory joint aches, with normal tests, and Western medicine had no idea what was going on with her. She had undergone an expensive medical workup, and the only recommendation was to take anti-inflammatory medications. A Buddhist herself, she was more than happy to get a non-traditional, un-American point of view.

Afterwards, she related this story.

Wearing his traditional red and yellow robes, Chagdud was waiting for her in the examination room, where two chairs had been set up. After exchanging pleasantries, Chagdud asked her to relax and began to take her pulse. For forty-five minutes, she and Chagdud sat quietly in a meditative state. No words were spoken, just the taking of the pulse and the meditation.

After this lengthy period of silence, Chagdud asked a single question. "Do you dream about snakes?"

She was shocked, as in fact, she did. Her backyard would overgrow during the summer, and when she mowed the grass, she might inadvertently run over a snake that would get chopped up and spit out the mower outlet. This horrified her, resulting in a surge of adrenaline and tingling that took some time to resolve, and resulted in recurring nightmares. Chagdud told her that her joint aches were due to the embodied tension engendered by the shocking and unexpected killing of another being. This was an explanation that made sense to her.

In America, Chagdud did not have access to the medicines he used in Tibet. In Tibet, he would roam the hills and collect parts of various medicinal plants. The same plant would have different effects and uses depending on which ecological niche it grew in – sunny, shady, protected, windy, high or low altitude, barren or lush. But in America, all he could prescribe was meditation and intention. In this case, he advised her to always be kind to snakes, and that whenever she saw a snake or snake home or hole, to always think kind thoughts about them. We never found out if her pains went away, but his intuition and suggestions were quite powerful, and provided a unique perspective on the origin of her malady.

Chagdud was an accomplished artist, traditional dancer, and singer. Tibetan ceremonies are often fantastic and dramatic – there is chanting, incense, clashing of cymbals, blowing of horns, throwing of rice, offerings being made, eating. But often in the midst of the magnificent cacophony and seeming confusion, a song will emerge, a special evocative mantra, where all is quiet but the singing. The first time I heard Chagdud sing a particular Tibetan mantra, the melody, intonation, and emotion of his voice produced shivers and tingles in my skin and scalp. It was a prayer of invoking wisdom beings, an ancient melody handed down over the centuries. It was powerful, melodic, timeless, vast, ancient, sad and happy at the same time, chilling, and deeply moving. Though I didn't know what the Tibetan words meant at the time, the song evoked emotions that I didn't know I had. I got the uncanny feeling that this song had been dormant within me and was now awakened. This prayer song seemed as important as anything I had ever heard. As soon as I heard it, I knew that this song was what I was meant to receive from my chance encounter with this astonishing person.

The Tibetan words to the mantra, sung over and over, are *Om Ah Hung Vajra Guru Padma Siddha Hung*. There are volumes written about the many-layered meaning of this mantra, which in rough English translation is, *With my entire being, I invoke the hearts and minds of past wisdom beings, to fill me with the realization of the true nature of reality, and to purify all negative influences and actions in myself and others.*

The reciting of the mantra, or prayer, is said to be useful in challenging times, to bring stabilization and peace of mind. The melody is haunting, and still gives me chills, and still when I sing it, in times of need, or when it seems I have lost my way – it is literally invoking the ghost-essence of the dedicated, kind, generous, and wise teachers of the past, who have said, with authenticity, *we are here to help.*

* * *

THIS WAS THE SONG I SANG IN MY CAR ALONG WITH Chagdud's recorded voice, holding him and Jane in mind, as I made the nine-mile journey up Marys Peak, on Memorial Day, to the Kalapuya place of spiritual power, for this final letting go. I paused in the parking lot at the base of the climb, collecting myself from the long drive. Then I started my last ride with Jane to the summit of Marys Peak. Tears flowed. It was difficult, but possible, to sing and cry simultaneously.

On arriving at the top, I was surprised to find we had Marys Peak to ourselves; there were no other visitors, which was unusual, but seemingly auspicious. Perfect. There would be no human audience for what was about to take place.

It was an overcast day, and the large meadow at the top was immersed in passing mountaintop clouds. It was chilly and breezy; the fir trees encircling the open arena were murmuring, whistling, swaying. Birds glided to their positions to watch.

Not really knowing exactly what I was going to do when I arrived at this special destination, it came to me, that I was to throw Jane's ashes into the moving flow of clouds, as if seeding them. From there, she would be taken into the sky, and as the ashes fell to earth, she would enter the watershed, and then the ocean. Clouds. Sky. Earth. Ocean.

I opened the box that had remained closed for four years, and while singing the mantra from my soul, and with steadily increasing fervor, depth, loudness, and confidence, I reached into the box and began to toss the ashes into the clouds, sending Jane on her way. I could see myself alone on the mountaintop, as I sang the haunting words and melody, my voice bathed in tears.

Then, something even more wondrous happened: as the ashes entered the clouds, the blowing wind began to dust me with ash. As I was letting go of Jane, she was dusting me with her essence. As I realized I was being covered with ash, I burst out laughing, and I continued until the box was empty, simultaneously laughing and crying, singing fervently, tears of sadness and happiness mixed, breathing in her remains, tears trickling rivulets through her sediment on my face. It was a powerful experience, this merging of love, loss, appreciation, and humor. It was the celebration of the coming together, then the coming apart, to come together again in some new and unknown way.

*　*　*

I will be forever thankful for being able to experience laughing and crying simultaneously. I think about it often. The bodily expressions of unbridled laughter and sobbing are similar: repetitive convulsive exhalations, guttural sounds, and tears. The body responds in similar ways to markedly different, seemingly opposite emotions. As Chagdud would say, they are of one taste.

I think of Chagdud and Jane often, especially when I see a rainbow, that perfect symbol of beautiful transience. They are both gone now, and are with me in a different way: Chagdud the mentor, Jane the lover. Remembering the mentor can be inspiring and easily bring happiness; remembering the lover can be difficult and easily bring sadness. That Memorial Day on Marys Peak I learned that crying and laughing were two closely linked ways of looking at the world, and that joy is not that far away from sorrow. I can grieve loss, and I can enjoy wonderful moments, and laugh with others. And when the storm clouds roll in, I can patiently wait for them to pass, and then enjoy the sunshine.

On Chateemanwi place of spiritual power, my soul sang a prayer for wisdom, and it was heard.

Undoing and Reassembly

I never imagined it would be this way. As a friend commented, this wasn't in the instruction manual.

When Jane died, I was in my late fifties and still working. My life had purpose. Her sudden and unexpected loss left me shaken, and all the traumas of my life began to build up and overflow through tears. It is a simple truth that how one grieves is personal and has no timeline. A year and a half after her death, whenever grief and sadness paid their regular and unwanted visit, I would still break down and sob uncontrollably. It seemed right to let it happen, to let it out. I knew it was a year and a half because I kept doing the math, asking, "How long will this last?" I'm not sure who I was asking, but the grief seemed bigger than me. My main solace was that I could find humor and affection between disabling bouts of sadness, and that when I was distracted, grief temporarily disappeared.

The night of her death, as I was crying myself to sleep, Jane came to me in translucent form, warm and naked, and embraced me. I could feel her touch. It was as real as life, and I was comforted, and thankful. This was the goodbye we missed, due to the suddenness of her death.

* * *

THIS WAS MY FIRST EXPERIENCE OF MAGICAL THINKING, termed so perfectly by Joan Didion. I could be riding my bike and a woman riding her bike at a distance would turn and smile, and it was her. Jane, what are you doing here? Where have you been? Where did you go? What have you been doing? Wait. Wait. Oh right. It couldn't be you.

Jane and I were avid birders and enjoyed visiting the beautiful and remote sites where birds flock and sing. I was the spotter; she was the identifier. Our special bird was the kingfisher. Coming out of nowhere, they would announce themselves with their characteristic call, gliding along a creek or stream, moving from one outpost perch to another, feeding along the way. They are audibly and visually distinctive birds, and it was always a special moment when a kingfisher appeared. The three of us were as one, a moment of aliveness and love. Wordlessly, we shared those moments of deep appreciation.

Not long after Jane's death, I glanced through a window in the backyard and saw a kingfisher! I was shocked, as kingfishers had no reason to be anywhere near our house, there being no water nearby. There was no doubt in my jangled mind that Jane had come to visit, to bring me peace of mind in the form of a kingfisher.

Minds can do strange things when traumatized. The day Jane died, she had been reading The Tibetan Book of Living and Dying. It was poignant to find it bookmarked on her bedside table, her imprint still on the sheets. She had been contemplating the next phase of her life, and in her transitional space, began meeting with a Buddhist group. We had never deeply shared our interest in Buddhism, and this promised to be a new phase of our lives.

Shortly after her death, two friends told me strange

stories—her sister Sarah, and Charlie, a bike riding acquaintance. Sarah called to tell me that Jane had come to her in a dream, to say "Don't worry, I'm ok, I'm still the same as I was before, only without a body. I'll still be around, only in a different form." There is a Buddhist metaphor that the space inside a vase is the same as the space outside; it is just separated by the shell of the vase. Tibetan Buddhists see the body as a temporary aggregate, a form, or shell, that emerges from a seed, and then dissolves and re-emerges in a different form, cyclically. Sarah was not familiar with Buddhism and had no way of knowing that metaphor. Yet that was Jane's message to her.

Charlie had a slightly different experience. A couple of weeks after Jane's death, he was riding alone on one of the beautiful roads leading to the countryside. He was on a stretch of road with a steep uphill that was a favorite cycling spot for Jane. She inevitably stood up out of the saddle as her heart and thunder thighs worked the hill, challenging the other riders. Everyone riding with her knew this was coming, but they always waited for Jane to make her move. This was her hill. As Charlie came to this part of the road, Jane appeared in the air next to him, as a robed and full-bodied, diaphanous and luminous vision. He was frightened, and tried not to look at her. He asked her out loud what she was doing here. "I'm fine," he told me she said. "I have left my body behind, but I am ok."

It was strange to hear these two similar stories, from people who had never met each other. I believe they felt obligated to tell me their unusual experiences because they thought I should know Jane was ok; they were just passing the message along. I wasn't worried about that. In keeping with Tibetan Buddhist ritual, every day for forty-nine days after her death I prayed for her essence to merge into the great wide open of light. Tibetans believe that when someone dies, they encounter the bardo, a between place where one's consciousness, still aware, disengages from their body. Their life's inclinations can make that a frightening experience or, with practice, an experience of death without suffering, a final, sublime event of ultimate merging. My prayers were that she would remain without suffering, and simply let go. I had no doubt she was ok. Nevertheless, I was shocked by the stories, and felt with conviction that there was another world out there, that on rare occasions could be glimpsed.

I pondered the meaning of this for years. I was also mystified as to why she appeared to them in that way, one in a dream, and one in a vision. I could understand Jane coming to me, but why did she appear to them, and with the same Buddhist metaphor? What did that mean? Whole religions are based on such appearances. It was unsettling.

My spiritual teacher, Chagdud Tulku Rinpoche, had died, so I couldn't ask him. It unnerved me, and remained a mystery for several years. Then I attended a Buddhist retreat with a teacher I felt might have an explanation. I told him the story of these appearances. "What does it mean" I asked, "to appear to people in the way that she did and saying what she said?" "It's not like that," he counselled. "Sarah and Charlie's experiences were their experiences, not yours. You are trying to understand them as if they are yours, and they are not." He inferred that the three of us experienced magical thinking – the appearances were real for each of us, but they were personal and unique experiences.

It seemed obvious when he told me that; I felt I should have been able to figure that out for myself. But I was living the mystery; I couldn't get around it, or above it. I was trying to construct a narrative that didn't exist. Realizing this turned out to be a relief, and a great example of the Buddhist encouragement to "drop the storyline," in order to obtain peace of mind. It is human to want meaning, but at its core, life is just experience.

*　*　*

I often consoled myself and others that Jane would still be with us, only in a different way, that our memories of her would always be with us. One way she remains with me is in my dreams. The night I wrote the first few paragraphs of this piece, Jane again came to me in a dream. I had not seen her in dreamworld for a while. She was telling me that she had to leave, vacationing with her family for a week, and that she had not invited me along, as she knew I would not want to spend a week with her six brothers and sisters, divorced parents, and decompensated mother. She was right about that. I guess it is not surprising that her dream being could read my mind.

For thirteen years, Jane and I have continued our relationship in dreamworld. We have literally grown older together, as I have watched her age, and gray. The dream theme is generally that she and I are now just acquaintances. She might have a boyfriend or be living with someone in a different setting. She had moved on, as she had with her death. Sometimes we would embrace, and though I could feel her warmth and suppleness, the pleasant feeling inevitably faded when I woke to discover it was a dream and had returned to waking reality. My dreams of her are as real as everyday life, leaving me to wonder if the dream reality is the true reality. Does my dream-self awaken me

Undoing and Reassembly　　　　169

only to send my body out for sustenance, so that I might return to the dream world? After a while, I accepted these dreams without strong emotion, the fact being, they were a nice break from the real world, and it was nice to see her.

＊　＊　＊

Life after Jane was a struggle, and a depression began to wear down my spirit. In my analytical way, I tried to read and think my way out of it, confident I would find a way if I could just identify and live the right perspective or philosophy. I finally concluded that the only way to overcome the loss of love, was to love. I would seek new and close relationships; I couldn't simply wait for love to come to me. "To save myself, I must love," I reminded myself silently. It took me years and experience to understand that this decision to love was really a mental "plan" to fix myself. It was not from the heart, where love lives, available and ready to be freed. I could not transfer my familiar love for Jane to new relationships, and it was noticeable.

I struck up friendships with two women who were longtime friends, and whose company I enjoyed immensely. They understood my situation and pursuit, and loved to engage in deep conversation, to have fun together, and to lie together. The pleasure was shared; they were experiencing their own losses. To me, there is nothing more soothing than a warm body to hold and be held by. When bodies wrap around each other in restful repose, the feeling is primal and enticing, the most naturally comfortable and restful place possible, far away from the activities and challenges of daily life.

Eerily, the two women independently expressed the same sentiment: they felt that I wasn't really with them, that I was with someone else. Though our togetherness was pleasant, as we probed deeper and grew closer, my thoughts seemed to be elsewhere. I sorely wanted these relationships to work, as I missed the joy of shared experience. But it appeared to them I was seeking the shared experience I had with Jane, while in truth I wasn't opening to a different shared experience with them. My intention to love was discernably the intention to love them in the same way as I loved Jane. With their courageous and helpful remarks, I became aware of these behaviors, and why they existed. I was thinking and daydreaming, and not simply being.

* * *

YEARS PASSED. NINE YEARS AFTER JANE'S DEATH, MY mother died at age ninety-nine. Yes, my mother the agent was still in my life. My mother and I had not really talked much in the years since I left home. I had moved as far away from my parents as I could, though I would visit occasionally, making sure that the stay would be no longer than three days. By the third day of 24/7 with my mother I needed to get away. She overwhelmed me just as much as an adult as she had when I was a teenager.

In her last years, being blind and frail, it was too dangerous for her to live alone. She agreed to a nursing home, where, as she put it, "I'll make the best of the hand I've been dealt." My sister and I were a perfect team – she lived a couple of hours away and would visit on weekends and take care of our mother's household matters and planning. My job was to manage the doctors, nurses, administrative staff, finances, and end of life decisions. Neither of us wanted to have anything to do with each other's job; it was a perfect division of labor. Mother was sharp until the end, and engaged in and directed every decision. She was still telling me what to do up to the day she died.

As she approached death, I bought a one-way ticket to Virginia to help manage the final days, the funeral and burial, and the sorting out of her estate. Decluttering her life was hard. Every day was full of tasks that exhausted me. Thoughts of Jane, and my struggle with relationships, took a back seat.

I returned home exhausted and resumed the effort of living life after Jane. But in the months that followed, my condition worsened. I completely lost my way. I was directionless and began wandering aimlessly, looking for what might come next. Life became surreal. I entered a coffee shop where I saw familiar faces, but no one seemed to recognize me, as if they were looking through me, making me wonder if I was really there. I had to embarrassingly ask a friend if I was alive, thinking that perhaps I had died, and this was all a dream. When was this going to end, and how? What was wrong with me?

One day I wandered into a bookstore, as reading continued to be a great distraction for me. I was browsing the titles in the far stacks and came across *Swamplands of the Soul.* That's me, I said to myself, that exactly describes my situation. I sat on the floor of the bookstore and began to read. The author, James Hollis, was speaking my language. At a time when my soul was lost in the depths, this chance discovery provided new insight and meaning.

Hollis is a Jungian analyst who had written several small pamphlet-like books packed not with advice, but with stories, and questions. I ravenously read many of his books, hoping to find answers to assuage my grief and loss of love, which at the time seemed to be the source of my misery.

I felt such a close connection with Hollis's writing, that I emailed him to ask if he could possibly speak to me about my condition.

Hello Dr. Hollis,

I am querying as to whether you do telephone or electronic consultations/analysis. I have found your books useful, and have attended two of your talks in Eugene, as well as attending one of your workshops. I feel your approach may be useful to me, thus my inquiry.

In short, I am a 66 year old retired family physician who has lost his way. Significantly, 8 1/2 years ago, my wife of 17 years was tragically and suddenly killed, run over by a fully loaded log truck while bicycling. It was a huge loss for me (and for our community), as she and I were what I guess you could call soul mates, one mind with two bodies, a unique relationship. I kept thinking time would heal, and it has some, but continues to affect my relationships going forward, there being daily triggers. I feel empty and desirous of connection and intimate companionship, but too much stuff comes up and I become overwhelmed. I do have a close inner circle of friends, and broad community support as I was a FP for 40 years in this community. Additionally, I retired a year ago and while happy not to have a schedule, I have a lot of time on my hands, and feel restless, immobile, and directionless. I am fortunate to have deep Buddhist training, but I am tired of just letting go, and feel I need to take some additional steps. I am by nature an introvert, and probably ruminate way too much, having self-analyzed myself for years, never having seen a therapist, and currently feeling at a bit of a loss, and increasingly tired, so I am a bit worried about myself. I have scheduled an appointment with a local therapist, but with someone I have no experience with. Because of the connection through your books and meeting you in Eugene, I have some feeling of connection with you.

To me, the wound feels traumatic, but that it brings up all the traumas of my life, rejections and blows to self-confidence, and there remain the trigger/reminders of my wife that continue to fire those neurons. Letting go helps relieve the symptoms temporarily, I am just looking for ways to deal with healing the wound and stop knocking the scab off. I don't seem to have the right outlet, or direction.

Ok, not so short, there is of course more, let me know if you have interest, and feel free to charge me your usual fee in response.

Thanks for your consideration, and I understand completely if your schedule does not allow such a conversation.

To my surprise, Hollis answered immediately. He was wrapping up his work in Houston and was moving to Washington, D.C., and as a result, had time on his calendar. He had never engaged with someone by telephone before meeting them personally, but my letter struck a chord with him. I would soon find out why.

On our first call, I anxiously began blurting out my complicated and messy narrative. I had only gotten a couple of sentences out when he interrupted me to say, "Stop. Before we go any further, I want to let you know that *I know how you feel.*" I immediately knew I was in the right place. He was the first person to say that to me. Over the years I had tired of the all-too-common polite and well-meaning remark, "I can't imagine how you feel." Here was someone who, based on an email, jumped right in to let me know he indeed *could* imagine how I felt, and *knew* how I felt. He too had lost a loved one, had struggled to find his way, and crossed that abyss.

We had regular telephone conversations for over a year, and I began to develop a new perspective. He pointed out that this latest downturn likely had more to do with my mother's death and my retirement, which had added to the trauma of Jane's death. After all, Jane had been gone for 9 years, and here I was newly decompensating. Of course. That had not occurred to me. Even though I had moved as far away from my mother as geographically possible and talked to her rarely, she had still been providing a life script, just as she had before I was a conscious child. Now that she was gone, and Jane was gone, and my occupation was gone, I no longer knew my role in life. I had no script. For the first time in my life, no one was telling me what to do. I could live my life as I pleased, yet I was unhappy. I didn't know what to do with myself. I was experiencing true freedom, but it was a terrible freedom.

I was stuck in sixty-eight years of habits, fortunate enough to have experienced love, and desperately searching for the same kind of love. I was bringing all my past scripts into relationships, and the play was bombing. I needed to let the scripts go. Furthermore, he queried, had I considered the importance of loving and caring for myself? If I didn't love me, and love to be me, how could I love someone else?

One night, unable to get to sleep, distraught in misery, I remembered the advice to love Tom. I intentionally consoled myself as I might a loved one. With ease, I imagined holding my head in my lap, stroking my hair and face, and comforting myself. As I quietly sang a song, a lullaby to my poor soul, I drifted into a peaceful sleep.

Breaking habitual thinking and behavior isn't easy. I'm seventy now, so there is no time left for laziness. Over time, with the help of those who love me, the terrible freedom has become true freedom, free from the prison of my own mind. It is the freedom of being, and I am now free to love again.

www.ingramcontent.com/pod-product-compliance
Lightning Source LLC
Chambersburg PA
CBHW071621030726
47598CB00001B/372